DORLING KINDERSLEY DK EYEWITNESS BOOKS

SHIPWRECK

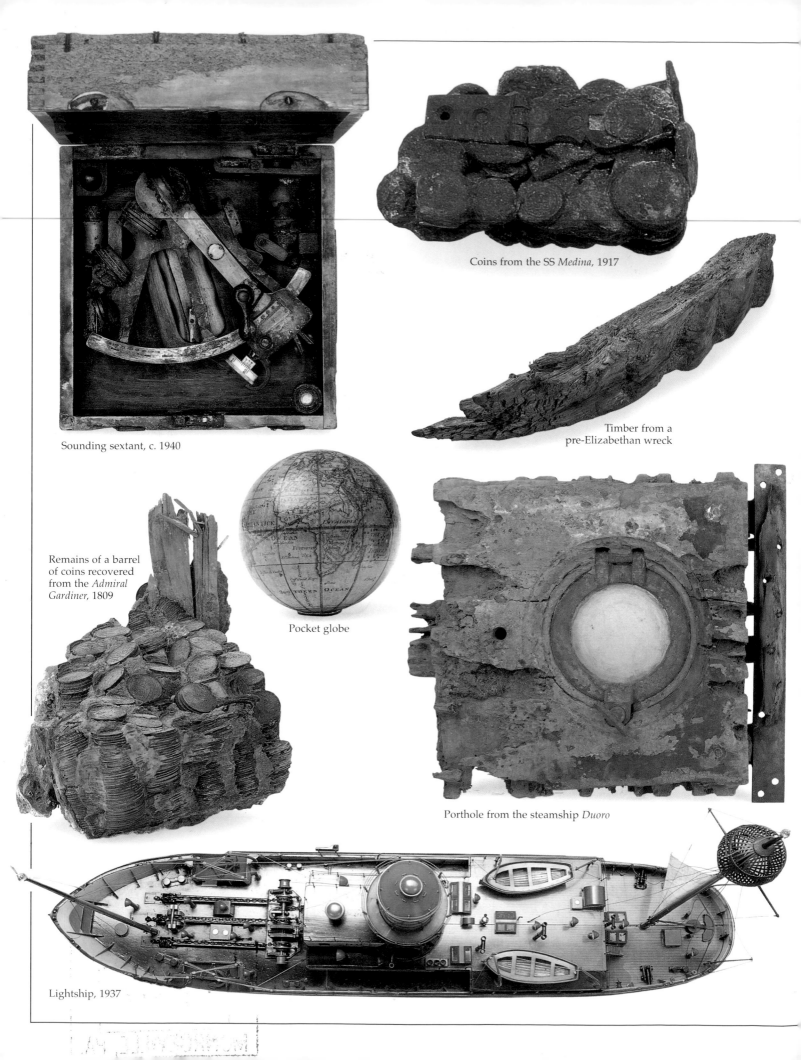

Sounding sextant, c. 1940

Coins from the SS *Medina*, 1917

Timber from a
pre-Elizabethan wreck

Remains of a barrel
of coins recovered
from the *Admiral
Gardiner*, 1809

Pocket globe

Porthole from the steamship *Duoro*

Lightship, 1937

Gold sovereigns
from *Ramillies*, 1760

Money weights
from *Santo Christo
de Costello*, 1666

Harmonicas
recovered from the
sea after 100 years

DK Eyewitness Books

SHIPWRECK

Written by
RICHARD PLATT

Photographed by
ALEX WILSON and
TINA CHAMBERS

Bottles from a
British ship,
wrecked in 1805

Lump of coins

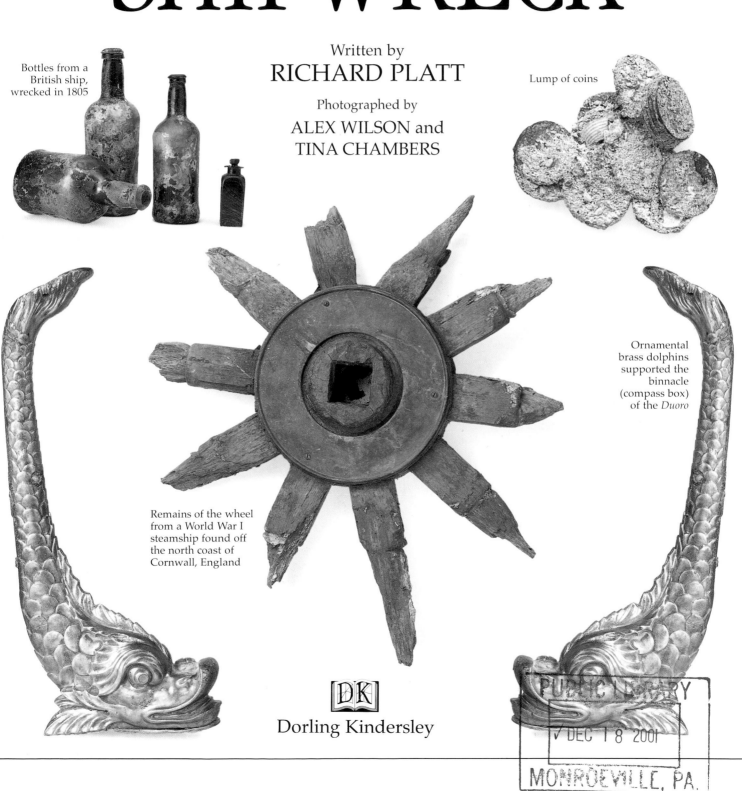

Ornamental
brass dolphins
supported the
binnacle
(compass box)
of the *Duoro*

Remains of the wheel
from a World War I
steamship found off
the north coast of
Cornwall, England

DK
Dorling Kindersley

Bell from the
Fresco, 1940

Flintlock pistol
found on the wreck
of *Hollandia*, 1743

Dorling Kindersley
LONDON, NEW YORK, DELHI, JOHANNESBURG,
MUNICH, PARIS and SYDNEY

For a full catalog, visit

DK www.dk.com

Project editor Melanie Halton
Art editor Ann Cannings
Designer Emma Bowden
Managing editor Linda Martin
Managing art editor Julia Harris
Picture research Deborah Pownall
Editorial consultant Richard Larn
Production Lisa Moss

This Eyewitness ® Book has been conceived by
Dorling Kindersley Limited and Editions Gallimard

© 1997 Dorling Kindersley Limited
This edition © 2000 Dorling Kindersley Limited
First American edition, 1997

Published in the United States by Dorling Kindersley Publishing, Inc.
95 Madison Avenue, New York, NY 10016
2 4 6 8 10 9 7 5 3 1

Dorling Kindersley books are available at special discounts for bulk purchases for sales promotions
or premiums. Special editions, including personalized covers, excerpts of existing guides, and
corporate imprints can be created in large quantities for specific needs. For more information,
contact Special Markets Dept., Dorling Kindersley Publishing, Inc., 95 Madison Ave.,
New York, NY 10016; Fax: (800) 600-9098

Library of Congress Cataloging-in-Publication Data
Platt, Richard.
Shipwreck / written by Richard Platt.
p. cm. — (Eyewitness Books) Includes index.
Summary: Describes the history of shipwrecks, famous wrecks, causes, navigation
and rescue techniques, underwater archaeology and the exploration of wrecks.
1. Shipwrecks—Juvenile literature. [1. Shipwrecks.] I. Title.
G525.P5283 2000 910.4 C52dc21
ISBN 0-7894-5885-3 (pb)
ISBN 0-7894-5884-5 (hc)

Color reproduction by Colourscan, Singapore
Printed in China by Toppan Printing Co. (Shenzhen) Ltd.

Model of
the *Mary Rose*

Ship's
signaling lamp

Tinplate box of matches
found on the wreck of the
Avalanche,
1877

Coins recovered
from beneath the sea

Contents

Coral on a bottle

Rocks, wrecks, and rescues

Aᴋ ᴘᴇᴏᴘʟᴇ ᴡʜᴀᴛ ᴀ ꜱʜɪᴘᴡʀᴇᴄᴋ ɪꜱ, and they will probably say that it is the sinking of a vessel, or its destruction on a rocky coast. Some may give a different reply: a shipwreck is the remains of a ship resting on the seabed. A sailor will have yet another opinion: "Why, it's the end of the world for those on board!" Or perhaps you will hear salty yarns of thrilling escapes or daring rescues; of castaways, sunken treasure, and unsolved maritime mysteries. An archaeologist is likely to think that shipwrecks are fascinating views of the past, frozen in time like stopped clocks. All these answers are right; a shipwreck can be many things to many people. The pages that follow offer a glimpse of all these possibilities.

SAVING LIVES AT SEA
When ships are wrecked near the shore, a lifeboat (pp. 40–43) speeds to the area of the disaster. The lifeboat crew plucks survivors from the ocean, or rescues them from the vessel if it is still afloat. A stretcher like this one is used to rescue the wounded without injuring them further.

Belts hold the injured securely in place

Rigid frame protects against bumps

Handles help lifeboat crew to affix stretcher to rescue line

DRAMA AND TRAGEDY
Ancient Greek writers chose shipwrecks as subjects as long ago as the 8th century B.C. Since then, the drama of a shipwreck has continued to fascinate writers and painters (pp. 58–59). Artist Samuel Owen painted this scene in 1837.

TREASURES FROM THE DEEP
Not all shipwrecks contain gold and silver in rotting chests! But treasure wrecks do exist, and the possibility of discovering a fortune lures countless divers to explore the seabed.

Forty boxes of Mexican liberty dollars were found on the Crescent City, *a steamship wrecked in 1871*

Flaps prevent an injured body from moving

ITALIAN TRAGEDY
Navigation equipment (pp. 32–33) reduces the risk of shipwreck, but it cannot eliminate the danger altogether. The *Stockholm*, which rammed the *Andrea Doria* (above) one foggy night in 1956, appeared as an approaching blip on the radar screen, but the Italian passenger liner could not turn quickly enough to avoid collision.

STEERING TO DISASTER
The sea can prevent human exploration of a wreck for many centuries, but it does not protect a vessel from marine life. Sea creatures, which can make a meal of woodwork, reduced this ship's steering wheel to hub and spokes over a period of 90 years.

AIR-SEA RESCUE
When a ship is in distress in the open ocean, aircraft can quickly scan vast areas. If they locate a life raft or floating wreckage, rescue helicopters (pp. 41, 43) take over, winching victims to safety. Air and sea rescue services cooperate closely.

STORMY WATERS
Gales wrecked countless ships in the days before steam power. A sailing ship driven onto a lee shore (a coastline facing the wind) had almost no way to escape being wrecked.

Wheel spokes eaten away by marine life

GHOST SHIP
Not every shipping disaster leads to a wreck; some end much more mysteriously. Cast adrift on the Atlantic Ocean, the sailing ship *Mary Celeste* was found empty but undamaged in December 1872. An abandoned meal lay on a table in the cabin, and the cargo of alcohol was untouched. Nobody has ever been able to explain what happened to the crew.

DIVING FOR PICTURES
The invention of scuba (pp. 46–47) in the 1940s made it much easier for archaeologists to study wrecks. This commercial diver is equipped to videotape his find with a head-mounted camera.

Hazards of the sea

THE SEAFARER'S LIFE is a dangerous one. Rocks may punch holes in a ship's hull; ice may crush it. Wind and surf can break up a ship, or fire can burn it to its waterline. These and many other hazards still destroy vessels large and small, even those that have strong steel hulls and powerful engines to help them steer clear of danger. If a shipwreck occurs, ocean waters quickly drown those unlucky sailors who are unable to reach a lifeboat. Swimming is a surprisingly modern skill, and many mariners lacked it. When the British naval ship *Lichfield* was wrecked in 1758, only 60 sailors out of a crew of 350 could swim. Often nobody on board could swim. One crew whose vessel ran aground had to tie a rescue rope to the ship's pig and let it swim them to safety. It is no wonder, then, that only half of all sailors died of old age. The sea, and countless other maritime hazards, consumed the rest.

WAVES
High winds whip up ocean waves of terrifying size. Waves are most likely to damage a ship at sea by swamping it with water – not by tipping it over. The pressure and suction of waves crashing against the shore breaks up any ship that runs aground.

BLOWING IN THE WIND
Buoys – floating markers – indicate the position of many known hazards to ships. A chain or cable anchors the buoy to the seabed, and its distinctive shape and color identify the hazard it marks. European nations introduced the first wooden buoys in the late 15th and early 16th centuries.

FOG
Sea fog forms when warm air blows across cold ocean water. Before the invention of radar, thick fog made navigation extremely hazardous. Helmsmen (steering officers) had to rely on the sound of foghorns and ships' bells to avoid running aground or collisions.

SANDBANKS
In shallow water, banks of sand can easily trap a ship as the tide goes out. Currents move sandbanks, so a ship's charts can indicate only roughly where they lie.

CORAL REEFS
In tropical regions, a coral reef – made of the chalky skeletons of marine creatures – surrounds many islands. The biggest ships anchor in deep water beyond the reef, but smaller vessels try to find a safe channel through the sharp barrier. Not all succeed.

WRECK BUOY
In narrow straits and shallow stretches of water, wrecked ships can themselves obstruct the channel, thereby increasing the likelihood that another wreck will occur. In the English Channel, one of the busiest shipping lanes in the world, there are the remains of more than 2,000 shipwrecks. Buoys mark the positions of the most dangerous ones.

EXPANDING ICE

Around the North and South Poles the ocean is permanently frozen. During the winter more seawater freezes to form pack ice (large masses of floating ice). Ships such as the *Pandora* (right), which was caught in the ice in 1876, are stranded there until the spring thaw. Drifting pack ice can create tremendous pressure – enough to crush and sink a wooden-hulled ship.

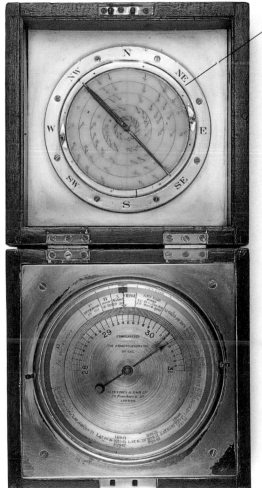

Wind disk for tracking the path of a typhoon

AVOIDING THE STORM

Since 1960 orbiting satellites have enabled meteorologists to track hurricanes and send warnings to ships. But weather forecasts were not always so dependable. In the past, mariners relied on instruments such as this "baryocyclometer." Its lower dial is a barometer that indicates air pressure. The upper dial suggests the safest course to steer, based on the wind direction.

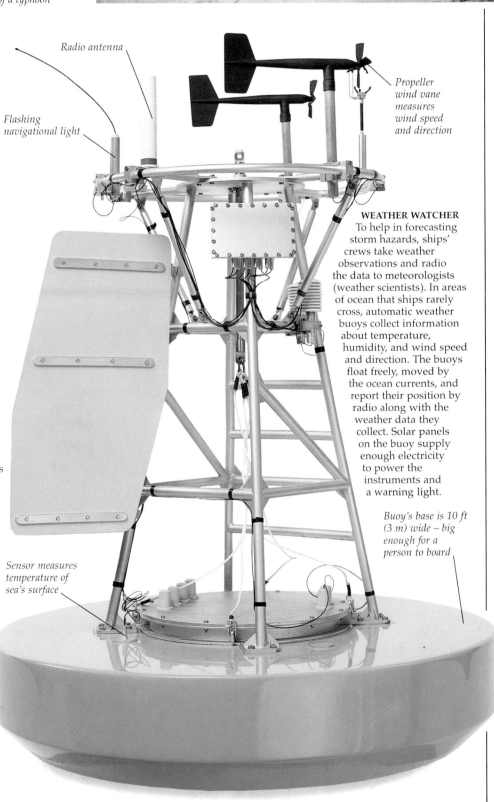

Radio antenna

Flashing navigational light

Propeller wind vane measures wind speed and direction

WEATHER WATCHER

To help in forecasting storm hazards, ships' crews take weather observations and radio the data to meteorologists (weather scientists). In areas of ocean that ships rarely cross, automatic weather buoys collect information about temperature, humidity, and wind speed and direction. The buoys float freely, moved by the ocean currents, and report their position by radio along with the weather data they collect. Solar panels on the buoy supply enough electricity to power the instruments and a warning light.

Buoy's base is 10 ft (3 m) wide – big enough for a person to board

Sensor measures temperature of sea's surface

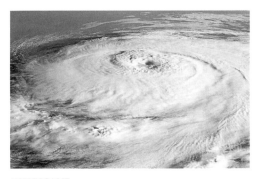

HURRICANE

Cyclone, typhoon, and hurricane all mean the same thing: a gigantic revolving tropical storm. Hurricanes bring torrential rains, winds as strong as 150 mph (240 km/h), and mountainous seas. Some are powerful enough to pick up yachts and throw them onto land.

Ancient wrecks

THE MARINERS WHO CROSSED the Mediterranean Sea more than 3,400 years ago set sail from at least seven great civilizations on its shores and islands. But whether these sailors spoke the language of Egypt, Cyprus, Greece, or some other country, the word for "shipwreck" had the same terrible meaning to all of them. Rocky coasts and violent storms sent many of their craft to the seabed. These Mediterranean wrecks are the oldest ever discovered. Their exploration has provided fresh knowledge about ancient Mediterranean cultures and the ships that supplied them. When the Ulu Burun wreck sank in about 1316 B.C., it was carrying enough copper and tin to make 11 tons of bronze. This, together with glass, perfumed resin, and gold valuables, suggests that the ship's cargo may have been a gift for a Bronze Age king or pharaoh.

Hull was saved from destruction by cargo of wine amphorae (jars)

Reinforcing ribs were added after shell was complete

ANCIENT SHIP REBORN
The Kyrenia wreck was remarkably complete. It included some deck planking and the mast step (the reinforced portion of the hull that supports the base of the mast). With the help of these details, modern shipbuilders created a seaworthy reconstruction of the ancient Greek vessel.

Replica of the Kyrenia ship

Hardwood pegs held planks together

KYRENIA HULL
The remains of a hull (ship's body) found off Kyrenia in Cyprus shows how Greek carpenters built cargo ships 2,400 years ago. A ridge along one edge of each plank fitted tightly into matching groove cut into the neighboring plank. A thousand years earlier, shipwrights had used the same technique to build the Ulu Burun ship.

ULU BURUN

In 1984, a Turkish diver searching for sponges found what was at that time the world's oldest known shipwreck. The metal ingots raised were the first of hundreds that archaeologists later recovered. Trinkets and amphorae (left) littered the wreck, which was named after its location – Ulu Burun.

Unknown goddess holds a gazelle in each hand

Gold-covered head

Gold bracelet

Medallion with Canaanite star design

CANAANITE JEWELERY

The discovery on the Ulu Burun wreck of trinkets and raw materials from Canaan (now part of Israel) gave historians a clearer view of ancient Mediterranean trade. They used to believe that merchants from Mycenae (an ancient Greek city-state) controlled shipping. However, jewelery, ingots, and glass from the wreck show that the Canaanites rivaled them.

PROTECTIVE GODDESS

A bronze statuette from the Ulu Burun wreck depicts a naked goddess. Her pose is typical of a blessing goddess and suggests that she was a sacred charm who protected the ship. George Bass, an American archaeologist who led the team raising the wreck, believes that the presence of the goddess statuette indicates that the ship sailed from Syria.

Bronze statuette

Ivory hinges

THE WORLD'S OLDEST BOOK

Ivory hinges held together the carved wooden panels of this writing board. Divers found it in a jar of pomegranates on the Ulu Burun ship. Its owner scratched out messages in the beeswax that covered the recessed inner surfaces. If the words had survived, it would be the world's oldest book.

First quests for wrecks

A SHIPWRECK IS A TRAGEDY for the families of those who drown. But it is also an expensive calamity for the ship's owner, or the merchant with goods in the hold. Recovering these enormous financial losses was the aim of the first desperate attempts to raise ships, or their cargoes. Shipwrecks in shallow water were easy to salvage. Swimmers who could hold their breath for a minute or more plundered the wreck before surfacing for air. Wrecks in deep water, however, were out of reach, and most rotted on the seabed until the invention of diving suits around 1830. Scientific study of wrecks underwater started a century later, but archaeologists only began to supervise divers and to record wrecks methodically in the 1950s.

FIRST DIVERS
With practice, divers holding their breath could reach depths as great as 165 ft (50 m). Often they returned from the seabed clutching not the pearls or sponges that they were seeking but treasure from a forgotten shipwreck.

VASA **SALVAGE**
Construction of the *Vasa* (pp. 26–27) warship cost a twentieth of all Sweden's wealth. When the ship sank in 1628, it was a huge loss. Divers working inside diving bells reached the wreck soon after the disaster and recovered many of the ship's valuable guns.

RAISING THE *ROYAL GEORGE*
Wrecks of warships held a fortune in cannons. One cannon could pay the wages of 20 sailors for a year. In 1782, the *Royal George* sank with 100 guns. There were several attempts to raise the ship and its cannons, but all failed. The wreck was blown up with explosives in 1848 to clear the English harbor that it blocked.

COLORFUL CANNONS
When the *Mary Rose* (pp. 18–19) sank in 1545, salvage divers traveled from Venice to try to rescue the wreck, but they found only a few guns. Nearly three centuries later, John and Charles Deane, using a pioneering diving suit of their own design, raised these cannons.

SUNKEN SPANISH SILVER
In 1702 an Anglo-Dutch attack at Vigo Bay (right), on Spain's Atlantic coast, sank a hoard of silver that has lured treasure seekers ever since. The silver was on board ships returning from Spanish colonies in America. The first expedition to find the lost bullion began in 1720. It was a failure – as were the 30 searches that followed.

PHILOSOPHER'S GLASSY STARE
Among the treasures that the Greek navy recovered from the Antikythera wreck (below) was this spectacular bust of a philosopher, complete with glass eyes. Unfortunately, the divers who found the wreck sold many smaller bronze statues before reporting their finds.

POSEIDON STATUE
When the net of a fishing boat fouled (caught) on the bed of the Aegean Sea off Cape Artemisium in 1928, divers went down to investigate. They found a spectacular life-size bronze statue of Poseidon, Greek god of the sea. The wreck has since been lost again.

Main sail is decorated with mythological beasts

ANTIKYTHERA WRECK
A sponge diver working off the Greek island of Antikythera in 1900 surfaced raving about rotting corpses. What he had actually seen were statues in the wreck of a Roman cargo ship, much like this model. A government search revealed art treasures – and a mysterious box of gears that may have been used to predict the moon's phases.

Main-brace supports the main mast

Far Eastern junks

FOR FOUR CENTURIES the largest, safest ships in the world carried vast cargoes of porcelain. These great vessels were not Spanish galleons or Dutch East Indiamen; they were Chinese junks. China has an ancient tradition of boat building, and by the 15th century Chinese shipwrights were making big oceangoing vessels. When the Chinese invented sternpost rudders (p. 17), Arab mariners copied the design and took it to the West. Watertight compartments stopped junks from sinking 700 years before European ships incorporated this crucial safety feature. By 1450, junks were as big and seaworthy as 19th-century European ships. Even these sophisticated Chinese vessels, however, could not avoid the sea's power, and many of their porcelain cargoes ended up on the seabed.

TRADING JUNK
The junk was an ideal vessel for trading on China's coast and in China's great rivers. Its flat-bottomed hull and lifting rudder made it easy to beach and allowed the junk to sail in shallow water.

POISON TESTER
Much of the cargo in the Sinan wreck was green-glazed earthenware that Europeans called celadon. Superstition held that the pottery changed color or broke if the food it contained was poisoned.

CARGO FROM THE SINAN WRECK
Venetian explorer Marco Polo (1254–1324) might have eaten from crockery very similar to this when he visited the court of China's ruler Kublai Khan. This cargo of porcelain was on its way from China to Japan when the Sinan ship carrying it was wrecked off Korea's coast around 1323.

FIGURES FROM THE DEEP
During the mid-1980s a fisherman's catch of porcelain off Vietnam's south coast led the state salvage company to a junk wrecked 300 years earlier. Named after the nearby port of Vung Tau, the junk had burned to its waterline before sinking. These white porcelain figures were part of its rich cargo.

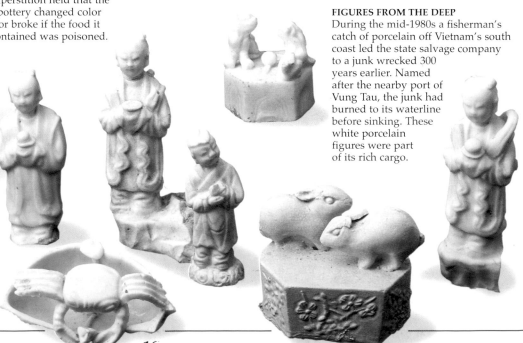

MAN–WOMAN GOD
A small pottery statuette raised almost intact from the Sinan wreck represents the Buddhist god Kuan-yin. This popular god was neither male nor female, so the figurine has a flowing female figure – and a bushy mustache!

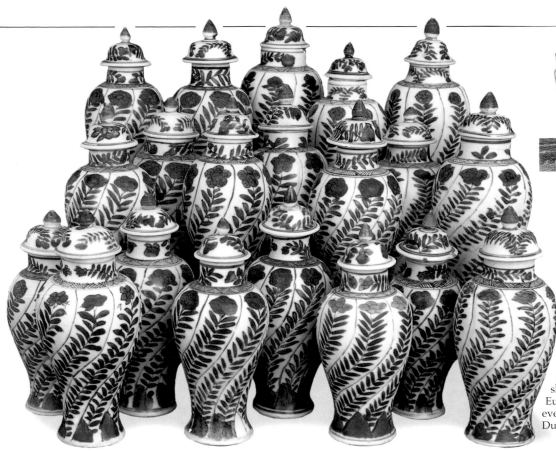

STERNPOST RUDDERS
The sternpost rudder on this Keying junk, made steering easy and safe because the rudder was in line with the ship's keel. European sailors used an oar hung over the ship's starboard side until they adopted this Chinese idea around 1200.

VUNG TAU VASES
Vietnamese divers recovered an astonishing quantity of porcelain from the Vung Tau wreck. Experts believe that the pots were among the first made in China specially for export to the West. Many of the shapes and patterns show signs of European influences – some vases are even patterned with houses similar to Dutch buildings of the time.

CHINESE PIRATE JUNKS
Not all junks traded peacefully. Chinese pirates armed their junks with small swivel guns and larger carriageguns that fired a ball as big as an orange. Fleets of as many as 700 pirate junks terrorized the South China Seas. Western nations policing the seas could not compete with them until they introduced paddle steamers. This illustration shows the British East India Company's steamship *Nemesis* destroying pirate junks at Anson's Bay in 1841.

TOWERING TEA BOWLS
The Vung Tau cargo sank around 1690, at a time when Chinese porcelain was fashionable and expensive in Europe. Within a century, however, European potters had discovered how to make thin, ceramic bowls like these for themselves. Inferior Chinese imports had also swamped the market, and ships brought porcelain from China only as ballast (to aid stability).

Raising the *Mary Rose*

O NE SUMMER'S DAY IN 1545, England's king, Henry VIII (1491–1547), stood watching his navy in the Solent, a sheltered channel on the south coast of Britain. The fleet, which included the second-largest ship in the navy – the *Mary Rose* – was setting sail to fight invading French ships. It should have been a simple, well-rehearsed routine, but on this day it was not. A breeze probably filled the sails before they were in place, and the *Mary Rose* heeled (tilted). When the lowest row of gunports dipped below the water, the ship was doomed. The sea rushed in, sinking the *Mary Rose* and drowning more than 650 sailors and soldiers, including the officer in command, Sir George Carew. Within minutes only the mast tops of this great ship were visible.

PORTRAIT OF A QUEEN
The *Mary Rose* was named after the king's favorite sister, Mary Tudor, and the royal flower emblem. The only surviving picture of the ship was painted the year after she sank. It shows a powerful, majestic, purpose-built warship.

Gunport on the main deck

Castle deck (ship's highest deck)

Small opening for swivel gun

ROYAL CANNONS
Henry VIII ordered shipwrights to build the *Mary Rose* in the first year of his reign as part of his effort to increase England's military might. To equip his enlarged navy with the brass and iron cannons it needed, Henry appointed a royal gun founder (caster). Henry's gun foundries used so much brass that in 1510 there was a world shortage of tin, which was mixed with copper to make brass.

Starboard side of the *Mary Rose*

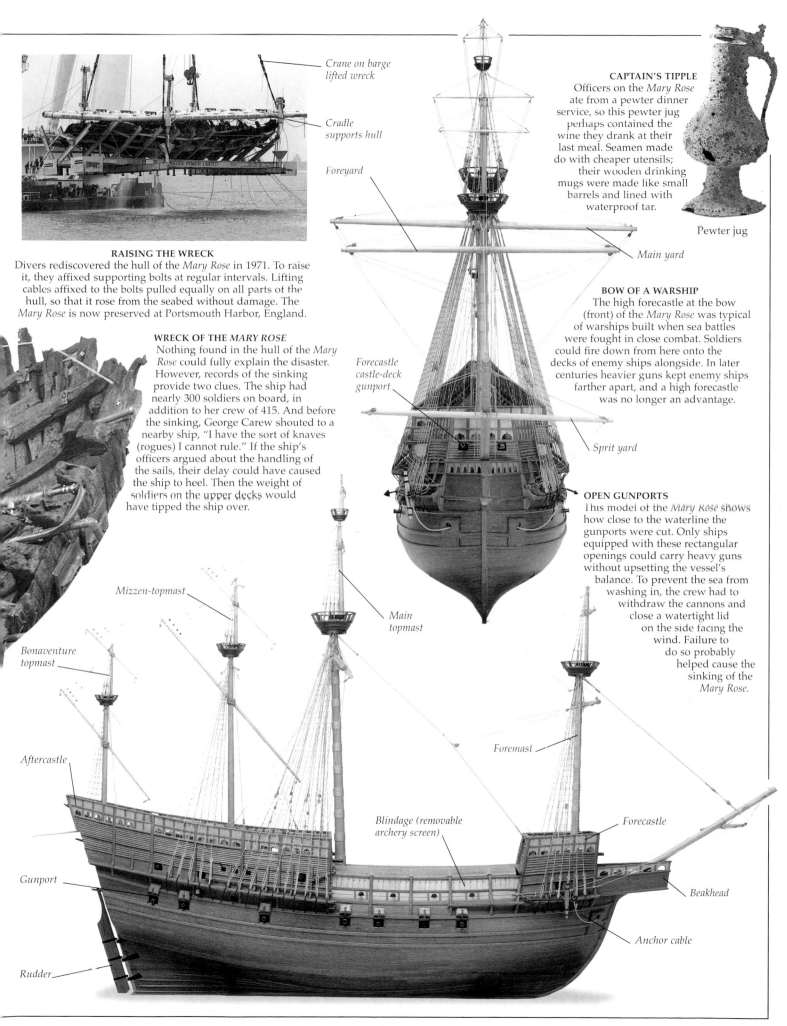

CAPTAIN'S TIPPLE
Officers on the *Mary Rose* ate from a pewter dinner service, so this pewter jug perhaps contained the wine they drank at their last meal. Seamen made do with cheaper utensils; their wooden drinking mugs were made like small barrels and lined with waterproof tar.

Pewter jug

Crane on barge lifted wreck

Cradle supports hull

Foreyard

Main yard

RAISING THE WRECK
Divers rediscovered the hull of the *Mary Rose* in 1971. To raise it, they affixed supporting bolts at regular intervals. Lifting cables affixed to the bolts pulled equally on all parts of the hull, so that it rose from the seabed without damage. The *Mary Rose* is now preserved at Portsmouth Harbor, England.

WRECK OF THE *MARY ROSE*
Nothing found in the hull of the *Mary Rose* could fully explain the disaster. However, records of the sinking provide two clues. The ship had nearly 300 soldiers on board, in addition to her crew of 415. And before the sinking, George Carew shouted to a nearby ship, "I have the sort of knaves (rogues) I cannot rule." If the ship's officers argued about the handling of the sails, their delay could have caused the ship to heel. Then the weight of soldiers on the upper decks would have tipped the ship over.

BOW OF A WARSHIP
The high forecastle at the bow (front) of the *Mary Rose* was typical of warships built when sea battles were fought in close combat. Soldiers could fire down from here onto the decks of enemy ships alongside. In later centuries heavier guns kept enemy ships farther apart, and a high forecastle was no longer an advantage.

Forecastle castle-deck gunport

Sprit yard

OPEN GUNPORTS
This model of the *Mary Rose* shows how close to the waterline the gunports were cut. Only ships equipped with these rectangular openings could carry heavy guns without upsetting the vessel's balance. To prevent the sea from washing in, the crew had to withdraw the cannons and close a watertight lid on the side facing the wind. Failure to do so probably helped cause the sinking of the *Mary Rose.*

Mizzen-topmast

Main topmast

Bonaventure topmast

Aftercastle

Foremast

Gunport

Blindage (removable archery screen)

Forecastle

Beakhead

Anchor cable

Rudder

British shipwrecks

BRITAIN'S LINKS WITH THE SEA are ancient – nowhere in Britain is farther than 73 miles (118 km) from the sea. Britain's coastal waters are treacherous, however, even for mariners who know them well. Jagged rocks and sucking sandbanks guard the shoreline. Some of the highest tides in the world wash the country's ports. Learning to escape these hazards made British sailors among the world's best, and by the 18th century Great Britain was a powerful maritime nation. A popular song, written in 1740, even claimed that "Britannia rules the waves." But no nation, however great, can ever really control the awesome power of the oceans, and British mariners knew they risked shipwreck on every trip.

DOWN THE HATCH
There is no reason to believe that drunkenness caused the wreck of the *Ramillies*, but all ships of the time carried plenty of drink. Officers often drank three bottles, or half a gallon, of wine a day. Seamen's fondness for grog (rum and water) earned it the nickname "the sailor's best friend."

Ramillies

The *Ramillies* was a first-rate man-of-war and one of the largest in the British navy. But when she made her last, ill-fated trip she was 96 years old and leaked badly. In February 1760, the *Ramillies* left the port of Plymouth in southwest England but on her return became trapped in Bigbury Bay, some 12 miles (20 km) to the east. There, hurricane-force winds drove the ship onto the rocks, killing 700 people.

Plate and spoons

Leather shoes

Buckles

WRECK REMAINS
Wreckage from the *Ramillies* filled Bigbury Bay, and local people sneaked off with anything that they could carry. Salvage work recovered some of the guns, but then the wreck lay undisturbed until 1906. Divers have since recovered hundreds of artifacts. A display of them at the Charlestown Shipwreck Center in St. Austell, Cornwall, creates a vivid picture of life on board the doomed warship.

ON THE ROCKS
Wind and waves snapped the masts of the *Ramillies* like matches, and flung the crew onto the rocks. The terrifying experience drove one officer completely mad; he stayed with the sinking ship and sang as it went down.

Royal Charter

The wrecking of the iron-hulled passenger and cargo ship *Royal Charter* (left) occurred in October 1859. The ship had just made a record run from Australia to Britain, but she could not compete with strong winds off the Welsh island of Anglesey which caused the ship to drift onto the rocks. One seaman swam ashore with a rescue line, but a huge wave broke off the stern of the ship, where most of the passengers were sheltering. Some of the 459 people who died in the wreck drowned because they jumped overboard wearing money belts full of gold nuggets.

Candleholder

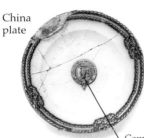

China plate

Company crest

Silver-plated teapot

Lid is stuck to handle

Duoro

Coffee, diamonds, and gold filled the hold of the mail ship *Duoro* as she steamed from South America to Britain in 1882. On April 1, just two days away from her destination, a collision with a Spanish vessel put a hole in the *Duoro*. Most of the passengers and crew escaped in the lifeboats, but her precious cargo sank 1,500 ft (450 m) to the bottom of the Bay of Biscay, off Portugal's coast.

China cup

Vase

Gold sovereigns

Duoro's compass support

"LOOK OUT!"
The *Duoro*'s small scuttles, or windows (above), did little to ventilate her cabins, and a passenger who went on deck in search of fresh air spotted the nearing Spanish ship. The crew ignored his warnings, with tragic results.

China plate

FINDING THE WRECK OF THE *DUORO*
A salvage team knew they had located the *Duoro* wreck in 1995 when they found a porcelain plate. Its sea-horse crest identified it as coming from a Royal Mail ship. The salvors raised 28,000 gold sovereigns from the bullion room.

Wreck of the Armada

SPANISH PEOPLE FELT SURE OF VICTORY when their navy set off to invade England in May 1588. They called the 130 warships the *Armada Invincible* – the unbeatable war fleet. When the ships reached England, however, the Armada's weapons could not match the cannons of the English fleet, and drifting fire ships (vessels deliberately set ablaze) forced the Spanish ships to scatter. Gales blew the Spaniards north and prevented them from picking up reinforcements. The Armada had to return to Spain by sailing around Ireland, where storms wrecked nearly 30 ships on the Atlantic coast. Four centuries later, archaeologists have excavated five of the wrecks. From gold trinkets – and ordinary items such as rigging – they are learning more about the ill-fated Armada and the lives of the 11,000 Spanish sailors who perished around British shores.

Gold and silver coins found on an Armada wreck

SPAIN'S RULER
Philip II, king of Spain from 1556 through 1598, ruled a vast empire, including the Netherlands. A revolt there threatened Spanish rule, so Philip launched the Armada hoping to end English support for Dutch rebels and to stamp out English piracy against Spanish ships.

Course the Armada ships were trying to steer

BREAKING THE RULES
The Spanish ships expected to fight by the traditional method of boarding English vessels to capture or destroy them. The English ships, however, had more cannons and defeated the Spaniards by firing from afar and avoiding close combat.

USELESS INSTRUMENT
The *Girona's* navigator would have used this astrolabe to check the ship's route by measuring the sun's position. But the Armada sailed home in fog and cloud, which hid the sun, and navigation errors led many ships to founder on the rocks.

ARMADA ROUTE
The Spanish fleet was first spotted on July 30, 1588, as it sailed into the English Channel, and was followed closely by English warships. On August 8, 1588, the decisive Battle of Gravelines broke out. Although defeated, the Spanish lost only two ships. Most of the losses came later, caused not by English victories but by shipwrecks.

TRAVELERS' CHAINS
Divers found eight gold chains on the *Girona* wreck. They were a very practical kind of jewelry: the links were unsoldered so that it was easy to detach a few to use in place of money.

HOLY CHARM BOX
When divers recovered this gold reliquary (holy relic box) from the *Girona,* it still contained an Agnus Dei (wax medallion bearing the stamp of a lamb, symbolizing Christ). These charms, made from Easter altar candles blessed by the pope, were supposed to protect those who carried them.

Loop of wire for attaching cross to a chain

Engraving of St. John the Baptist

Surface of cross was once covered in white enamel

ST. JOHN'S CROSS
This elaborate gold crucifix would have belonged to one of the wealthy officers traveling on the *Girona.* For the Spanish Catholics who sailed in the fleet, the Armada was in part a religious mission – England was a Protestant nation.

Severe weather and lack of food and water caused intense suffering as the Armada navigated around Scotland

Wreck of the Girona

Battle of Gravelines

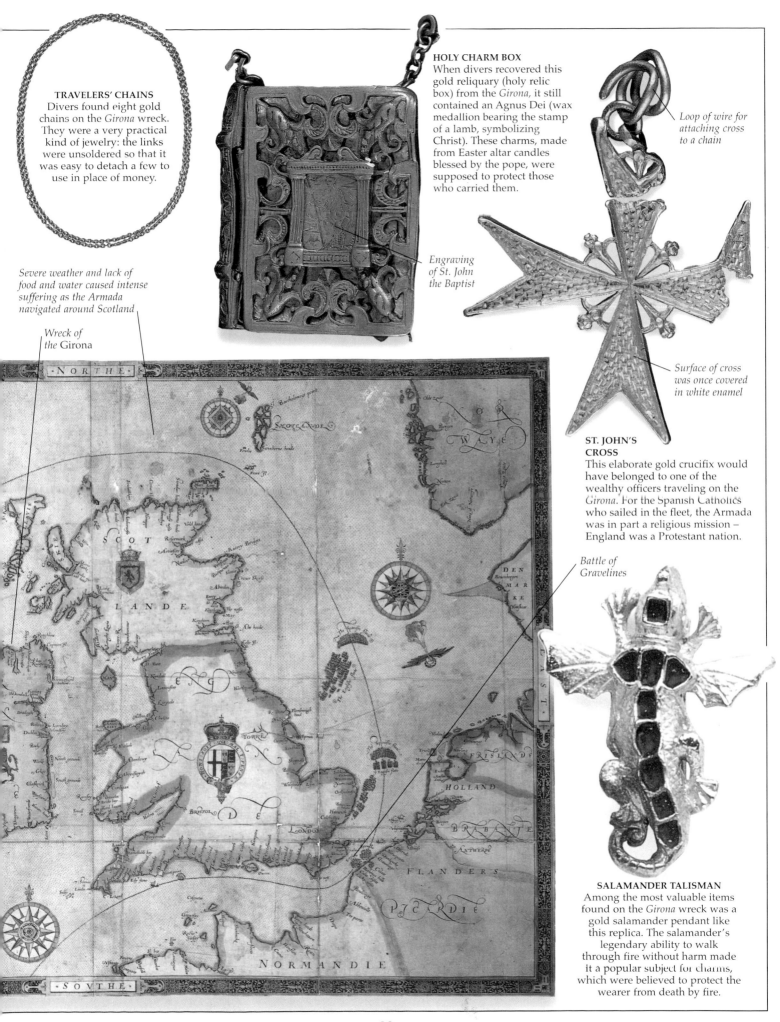

SALAMANDER TALISMAN
Among the most valuable items found on the *Girona* wreck was a gold salamander pendant like this replica. The salamander's legendary ability to walk through fire without harm made it a popular subject for charms, which were believed to protect the wearer from death by fire.

Lost in Lake Ontario

IN TERMS OF POWER, the United States Navy was a minnow to Britain's shark when the two countries went to war in 1812. The British navy had 800 warships; the Americans had only 16. The United States hurriedly built ships and also converted merchant vessels, including the Great Lakes schooners the *Hamilton* and the *Scourge*. Both of these schooners were more used to carrying coal than cannons, and they made poor warships. The weight of a cargo low in the hold helps to make a ship steadier; heavy cannons on the deck have the opposite effect. "It'll be our coffin," cursed the crew of the *Scourge,* and a squall in 1813 proved them right. The wind turned both the *Scourge* and the *Hamilton* over in an instant, and they quickly sank, killing all but eight of the crew from the two ships. The icy waters of Lake Ontario hid the ships until 1975, when a remote-controlled camera recorded these remarkable images of the lost schooners.

THE WAR OF 1812
The United States fought·Great Britain from 1812 to1815 to prevent British interference with American trade with Napoleonic France. They also wanted to put a stop to the British navy's practice of removing British sailors from American ships and forcing them back into naval service.

Hamilton
figurehead

LADY HAMILTON
Until she joined the navy, the *Hamilton* was called the *Diana*, and her figurehead shows a graceful 19th-century lady. The fresh, cold water of Lake Ontario preserved much of the intricate detail of the carving.

SHADOWY SHIP
Side-scan sonar (p. 50) provided this ghostly image of the *Hamilton* wreck. The ship stands upright on the bed of the lake, with its hull fully intact. The sonar "shadow" clearly shows the schooner's two masts, and outlines on the deck indicate the positions of hatches, cannons, boats, and other equipment. A research vessel from the Canada Center for Inland Waters made the image after locating the ship in 290 ft (88 m) of water.

SUBMERGED *SCOURGE*
A remotely operated underwater vehicle (ROV) photographed and videotaped the wrecks of the *Scourge* and the *Hamilton*. This artist's reconstruction, drawn from the pictures and video footage, shows the ROV at work above the *Scourge*. Many of the details it recorded are featured in a dramatic account of the sinking written by Ned Myers, one of the eight survivors. He described it to the American novelist James Fenimore Cooper in 1843. Cooper made the *Scourge* wreck a highlight of his biography *Ned Myers; or A Life Before the Mast.*

FIGUREHEAD FOR THE FOE
The *Scourge* had been a Canadian merchant vessel called *Lord Nelson* before she was captured by the United States and converted into a warship. The figurehead of Admiral Horatio Nelson, a British naval hero, led the *Scourge* into attacks on British ships! Although this sculpture has two arms, Nelson actually lost an arm during a battle 15 years before this ship was built.

Nelson leads the Scourge *into battle*

Figurehead of the
Scourge warship

***HAMILTON* SMASHERS**
Nicknamed "the Smasher" by British crews who faced it, the carronade was a short gun that could do terrible damage when ships fought at close range. The *Hamilton* carried eight carronades. The 18-lb (8-kg) iron balls that each gun fired were roughly three quarters the size of a bowling ball. The ROV's camera picked out this carronade's barrel resting on its mounting on board the *Scourge*.

Unveiling the *Vasa*

MARINERS KNOW that their voyage is always in danger of ending suddenly if they are shipwrecked, but for the crew of the *Vasa* the end came almost as soon as their vessel was launched. This magnificent sailing ship was to be the pride of the Swedish navy. On August 10 1628, the *Vasa* set out across Stockholm harbor on her maiden voyage. Shortly after the crew had raised the sails and the ship had traveled just 4,625 ft (1,300 m), a gust of wind blew the ship over. Within minutes the *Vasa* sank in 110 ft (33 m) of water. Three centuries later, archaeologists turned this tragedy into triumph. The wreck they raised in 1961 is the most complete example of a 17th-century naval vessel ever to have been discovered.

TOP-HEAVY WARSHIP
The *Vasa* had far too much weight above the waterline. She could stay upright in the sheltered harbor, but the slightest breeze was enough to capsize the top-heavy gunship.

SAILOR'S LAST MEAL
The wreck contained sad details of life on board. Seven messmates would have used these wooden spoons to eat their meals of porridge from a single shared bowl. Officers ate from pewter plates.

Traces of red paint can be seen on the jaws

SUNKEN GRAVEYARD
Divers found 25 skeletons in or near the *Vasa* when they began to explore the wreck. Many lay where they had fallen at the time of the sinking – one man was trapped under a heavy gun carriage. Divers also retrieved clothes and shoes with the bodies of the seamen. The coldness of the northern harbor, and the low salt content of the Baltic Sea, had prevented the fabrics and leathers from rotting. In addition to the garments that the seamen were wearing, more clothes were found packed in wooden chests on the decks where they were to live, work, and sleep.

SKELETON CREW
The full crew would have numbered 145, and the ship would also have been carrying 300 soldiers. But there was a reduced crew of 100 for the maiden voyage, as well as some wives and children. The sinking drowned at least 50 people. Even the admiral had a narrow escape. The disaster would have been very much worse, however, if the *Vasa* had actually gone to sea.

TAKE A BOW

The discovery of the *Vasa* put an end to arguments about how shipwrights built 17th-century warships. Especially controversial was the ship's beak – the pointed section sticking out at the bow, with the figurehead at its tip. Oil paintings of the time showed warships with huge ornamental beaks, but many maritime experts believed that the artists had exaggerated their size. The discovery of the *Vasa* proved that the experts were wrong. After the ship had been reconstructed, she really did have a gigantic beak, decorated with carvings of 20 Roman emperors on parade.

Beakhead

DISCOVERY AND RAISING OF THE *VASA*

A Swedish engineer and naval historian, Anders Franzén (born 1918), discovered the *Vasa* in 1956. A diver confirmed the location, and Franzén began a campaign to raise the wreck. Divers passed lifting cables under the hull, and salvage ships then pulled on the cables to raise the *Vasa* to the surface. Blocking the gunports and other holes in the ship's hull made it watertight, so that once pumps removed the water inside, the *Vasa* floated again.

Golden brown paint still visible on the lion's mane

SINKING SCULPTURE

To decorate the *Vasa*, woodcarvers sculpted 500 figures and 200 other ornaments from oak, pine, and lime woods. Mostly they chose mythical beasts, historical personalities, and Bible stories as their subjects. But they also carved mermaids, which superstitious seamen believed would protect them on a voyage. Unfortunately, the reverse was true. The weight of the many carvings almost certainly made the *Vasa* more top-heavy and helped to capsize the ship.

ROYAL CREST

The Swedish national emblem decorated the stern of the *Vasa*. Carvers built it from 22 separate pieces. Like many other carvings fixed to the ship, the crest still had traces of the golden brown paint that once made it gleam majestically.

GLOOMY GUN DECK

The lower gun deck of the *Vasa*, with its low beams and dark timbers, was completely reconstructed. Conservators replaced the gun carriages where they were found, but 17th-century salvage divers had removed the guns that they once supported.

"Unsinkable" *Titanic*

ICEBERGS MAKE THE NORTH ATLANTIC a fearsome obstacle course in the spring. Some icebergs tower as high as large office buildings above passing ships, but nine times as much ice floats unseen below the surface of the sea. Passengers on the *Titanic*'s maiden (first) voyage in April 1912 had no reason to fear icebergs. Everyone thought the *Titanic* was the safest ocean liner in the world – it was certainly the largest and most luxurious. Sadly, it was not "unsinkable," as the passengers believed. During the night of April 14–15, an iceberg buckled the steel hull of the *Titanic* below the waterline. Seawater rushed in and the ship sunk in less than three hours. More than 1,500 people died in the world's most notorious shipwreck.

LAUNCHING A DOOMED MONSTER
The *Titanic* was built in Belfast, Northern Ireland, in 26 months. The ship was launched on May 31, 1911. To make it as safe as possible, the ship's hull was divided into watertight compartments. Even if a hole allowed two compartments to fill with seawater, the *Titanic* would still float, but the iceberg that sank it pierced five compartments.

FASTEST HOTEL AFLOAT
Even though the *Titanic* was one of the fastest liners afloat, the trip across the Atlantic took more than four days. Passengers traveled in surroundings as comfortable as any fine hotel.

WRECK OF THE *TITANIC*
The *Titanic* broke in two and sank in 13,000 ft (4,000 m) of water – well beyond the reach of divers. The wreck was lost until 1985, when a vessel from Woods Hole Oceanographic Institution in Massachusetts found it using the remote-controlled submersible *Argo*. Model makers created this reconstruction of the wreck from photographs and video footage taken by the submersible.

TELEGRAPH OPERATOR
Radio operator Jack Phillips was so busy sending passengers' messages that he failed to pass on to the captain a vital iceberg warning he had received. When the *Titanic* began to sink, however, Phillips's SOS signals (p. 36) summoned help quickly. The *Titanic* disaster proved the value of radio in lifesaving at sea, and soon all ships carried the equipment.

TOO FEW BOATS
Though the *Titanic* could carry 3,511 people, there was space in the lifeboats for only a third of them. As a result of the wreck, international shipping laws changed to require that all vessels provide lifeboat space for every single passenger and crew member.

FRENCH SUPER-SUB
In 1987 a French team sailed to the *Titanic* shipwreck. Using the mechanical arms of the submarine *Nautile*, its crew lifted hundreds of objects. Survivors of the wreck and relatives of the dead attacked the expedition as sinister souvenir hunting.

Bitts, or bollards, for attaching cables, still stand on the deck

ON DECK
The coldness of the Atlantic water did not protect the *Titanic* from damage, as many had hoped it would. Marine worms have consumed most of the ship's ornate woodwork, and rust hangs in festoons from steel equipment.

Deck has collapsed where elegant glass dome once stood

Gate still closed between third-class and first-class areas

WINDOW ON A WRECK
The Woods Hole team returned in 1986 and dived to the *Titanic* in the deep-sea submersible *Alvin*. Cameras on board photographed much of the wreck, including this stateroom window.

Cargo crane

BURIED BOW
The ship's bow sank fast enough to plow itself 60 ft (18 m) deep into the seabed, and this deck rail now projects only slightly out of the mud. Concretions (p. 56) on deck equipment have made them resemble a figurehead, though the *Titanic* did not carry one.

Anchor crane

Oil tanker disasters

THE SHIPS THAT CARRY OIL are the biggest in the world, and their size makes them difficult to control. A ship needs several times its own length to turn, and oil tankers can be as long as 20 tennis courts. If they run aground, crude (unrefined) oil is often spilled. The oil floats on the surface of the water, forming a slick – a black, tarry layer. A slick coats everything it touches, polluting beaches and covering seabirds and mammals. The biggest tankers carry enough oil to fill 300 full-length swimming pools. Risking a spill of this size may seem like a dangerous environmental gamble, but the tanker cargoes are vital to heat our homes and run our cars. To reduce the danger of spills, new tankers must now be fitted with a double skin (a hull within a hull).

STRANDED TANKER
When the engines of the *Braer* failed in January 1993, the tanker drifted helplessly. Heavy seas prevented tugs from towing the *Braer* to safety. The tanker ran aground on the jagged rocks of Scotland's Shetland Islands.

ALASKAN SPILL
Pumping out oil from the grounded *Exxon Valdez* tanker helped to limit the damage to Alaska's coastline in 1989. The cleanup operation was problematic because of freezing temperatures and the site's remoteness; one sixth of the cargo (about 10 million gallons) escaped anyway. The spill seems huge, but industries and refineries in the United States consume this quantity of oil every 22 seconds.

CONTAINING THE SLICK
Oil coats only the surface of water, so it is possible to prevent a slick from spreading by blocking its path with a boom (long floating barrier). Workers in Wales launched a boom to contain the slick that spread from the *Sea Empress* after it ran aground in 1996.

TANKER INFERNO
When a tanker runs aground and cannot be refloated, pollution experts first try to pump oil from its tanks. If this is impossible, they may consider deliberately setting fire to the tanker to burn off the oil. Fires also start accidentally, though all tankers have fire control systems to prevent this. Tankers make easy targets during wars, and burning them deprives an enemy of vital supplies.

BEACH HOSES

Washing oiled beaches with high-pressure hoses forces some of the oil back into the sea, where it is easier to scoop up. This makes the sand look clean, but some experts believe that it prolongs pollution by driving the oil deeper into the beach.

OILED BIRDS

Spilled oil quickly covers the plumage of the marine birds that swim on the ocean and feed on the fish that live in it. The oil clogs up the birds' feathers, weighing them down and leaving them unable to fly. Birds peck at their feathers to clean themselves, and the oil that they swallow as a result may poison them.

BIRD BATHS

Capturing oiled birds and washing their feathers with detergents helps to remove the oil. When they have recovered, the birds are released. However, experts disagree about the effectiveness of cleaning. Recent research suggests that many birds die within a few weeks of release.

THE COAST IS CLEAR

The ocean environment gradually cleans itself after an oil spill. About a third of the oil evaporates within two days. Waves and sunlight eventually break the remainder into tiny drops that microorganisms can destroy. Cleaned mammals and birds, such as these penguins, can return to the wild within months of a spill.

COASTAL CLEANING

Cleaning an oiled coastline can be an enormous task. When the tanker *Exxon Valdez* ran aground on Alaska's Bligh Reef in 1989, its cargo polluted 1,250 miles (2,000 km) of coast. As many as 11,000 people helped to repair the damage. One of their tasks was to remove pebbles one by one for hot-water washing.

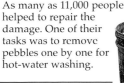

Navigation

THE FIRST SAILORS NAVIGATED by following the coastline. This was slow going, however, and rocks or shallows were never far away. When mariners sailed out of sight of land some 4,500 years ago, they followed the stars or the wind's direction—the compass was not invented until the 12th century. Sailors calculated distance from their speed and sailing time. They also drew charts and maps to help them navigate. These methods, however, were not precise enough to avoid wrecking on distant shores. So navigators learned to judge latitude (how far north or south of the equator they sailed) by measuring the sun's position. A simple way of finding a ship's position in an east-west direction (longitude) was invented in 1761.

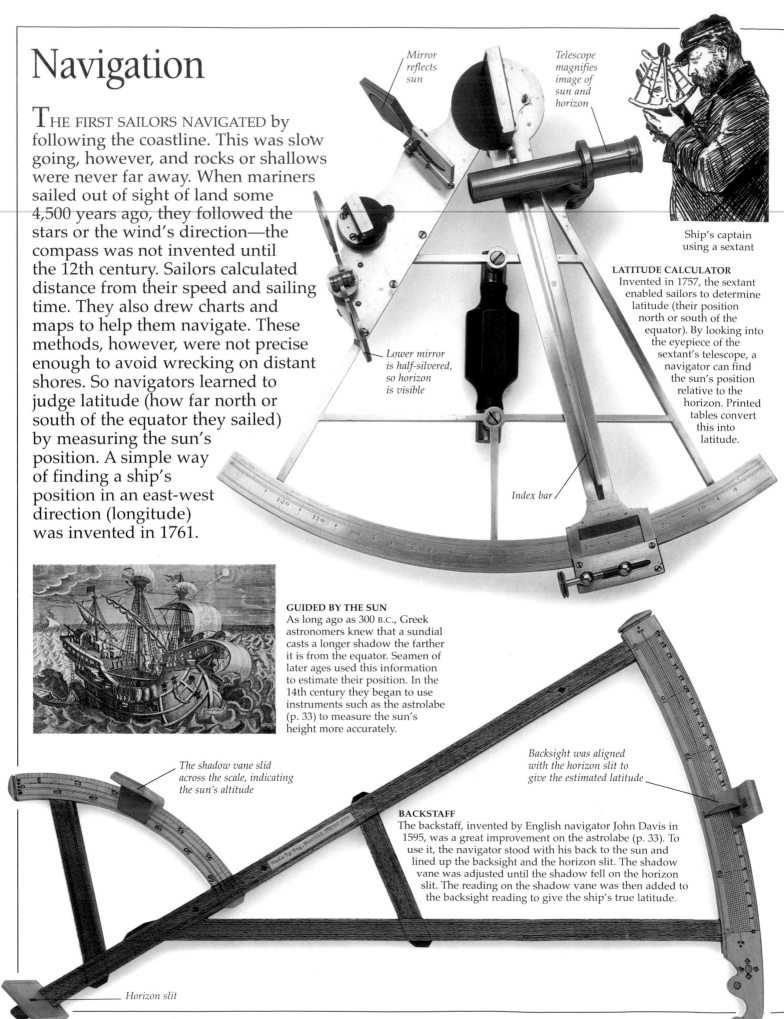

Mirror reflects sun

Telescope magnifies image of sun and horizon

Ship's captain using a sextant

LATITUDE CALCULATOR
Invented in 1757, the sextant enabled sailors to determine latitude (their position north or south of the equator). By looking into the eyepiece of the sextant's telescope, a navigator can find the sun's position relative to the horizon. Printed tables convert this into latitude.

Lower mirror is half-silvered, so horizon is visible

Index bar

GUIDED BY THE SUN
As long ago as 300 B.C., Greek astronomers knew that a sundial casts a longer shadow the farther it is from the equator. Seamen of later ages used this information to estimate their position. In the 14th century they began to use instruments such as the astrolabe (p. 33) to measure the sun's height more accurately.

The shadow vane slid across the scale, indicating the sun's altitude

Backsight was aligned with the horizon slit to give the estimated latitude

BACKSTAFF
The backstaff, invented by English navigator John Davis in 1595, was a great improvement on the astrolabe (p. 33). To use it, the navigator stood with his back to the sun and lined up the backsight and the horizon slit. The shadow vane was adjusted until the shadow fell on the horizon slit. The reading on the shadow vane was then added to the backsight reading to give the ship's true latitude.

Horizon slit

Hands showed correct time even when storms rocked the ship

Alidade (sighting rule)

Astrolabe from a wrecked Armada ship (pp. 22–23)

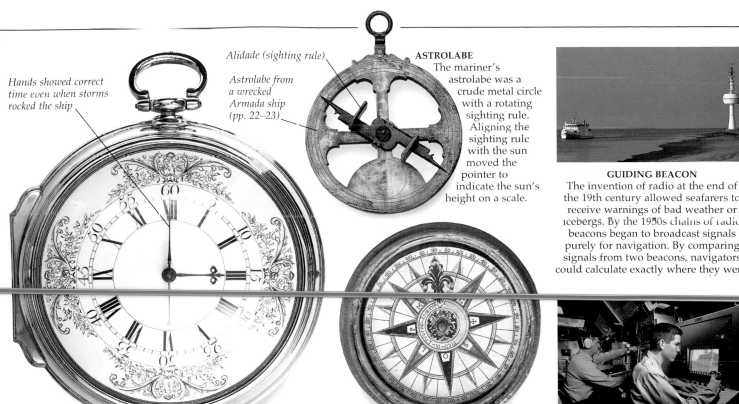

ASTROLABE
The mariner's astrolabe was a crude metal circle with a rotating sighting rule. Aligning the sighting rule with the sun moved the pointer to indicate the sun's height on a scale.

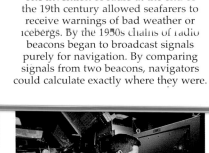

GUIDING BEACON
The invention of radio at the end of the 19th century allowed seafarers to receive warnings of bad weather or icebergs. By the 1950s chains of radio beacons began to broadcast signals purely for navigation. By comparing signals from two beacons, navigators could calculate exactly where they were.

CLOCKS SHOW THE WAY
In 1759 English clockmaker John Harrison built a chronometer that measured time accurately enough for navigation. The sun rises two seconds later each day for each 0.6 mile (1 km) that mariners sail west, so the change in time when the sun is directly overhead is a precise way to calculate longitude.

MAGNETIC MIRACLE
Balanced on a central pivot, or floating in liquid, the magnetized needle at the heart of a compass always turns to point north. Chinese navigators were the first to guide their ships with the aid of a compass around 1100.

RADAR STEERING
Radar helps to guide mariners in the fog or dark. The equipment broadcasts a radio signal and measures the strength of echoes. Radar screens show nearby ships, buoys, or coastlines as bright shapes.

Computerized chart plotter

GPS receiver

Sonic depth finder

Radar screen

ON THE BRIDGE
Around the wheel of a modern ship are radar screens, computerized charts, and other navigational aids. A receiver for signals from global positioning satellites (GPSs) gives the helmsman accurate readouts of the ship's position.

Guiding lights

THE POWERFUL FLASHING BEAM of a lighthouse or lightship warns sailors that they should beware of rocks or helps guide them safely into harbor. When ocean fogs make the lighthouse invisible, its mournful horn sounds a warning. Hilltop beacons first warned of danger about 3,000 years ago. By A.D. 400, Roman ships sailing from the Black Sea to the Atlantic were guided by 30 lights. These early beacons were wood fires burning on headlands or in sheltered harbors. In the 18th century, however, better building methods and reliable oil lights made it possible for lighthouses to stand on the rocks themselves. By 1820 there were 250 lighthouses worldwide. Lighthouses are not as important today as they once were, since radar and sonar help all but the smallest boats navigate in darkness or fog.

NORE LIGHTSHIP
A ship with a light can warn of danger in a spot where a lighthouse would be impossible to build. The first such lightship dropped anchor in the estuary of England's Thames River in 1731. It warned of the dangerous Nore sandbank.

Twin lanterns each held two candles

PHAROS OF ALEXANDRIA
The first true lighthouse guided ships into the port of Alexandria, Egypt. Called the Pharos, after the island on which it stood, the lighthouse was as tall as a modern 25-story building. A spiral ramp led to the top. Built around 280 B.C., the Pharos stood for 1,500 years.

LIGHTHOUSE HEROINE
When a ship founders, the lighthouse keeper is often the first to know – and the first to attempt a rescue. When the *Forfarshire* ran aground off England's northeast coast in 1838, the lighthouse keeper and his 23-year-old daughter, Grace Darling, risked their lives to save survivors. Grace's bravery made her a popular heroine of the day.

LIGHTSHIP
Until about 1820 all lightships were adapted from fishing boats or merchant ships. Later vessels, such as this one from the 1930s, were specially built to carry a light. Lightships were dangerous to crew and expensive to maintain. Many lightships have been replaced by buoys, and those that remain are now automatic and therefore need no crew.

Beacon

Lifeboats

Anchored lightships over 100 ft (30 m) have to show a "black ball" during daylight hours. If a ship's position becomes unreliable because of severe storms, the "ball" must be lowered.

Foundations are sunk as deep as 150 ft (45 m) into the seabed

PILE LIGHTHOUSE
Where a solid masonry lighthouse would be difficult to build, a steel pile structure similar to an offshore oil rig can support the light on top of a lattice structure.

SOLITARY LIFE
All lighthouses once had keepers. They lit the lamp at dusk and put it out at dawn, cleaned the lenses, and operated the horn in fog. It was a lonely and often boring job. Since most lighthouses today are automatic, few need crews to operate them.

BRILLIANT BULB
This giant electric light bulb is for use at the top of a lighthouse. It produces a warning beam as bright as about 50 domestic light bulbs. A curved reflector behind the lamp helps to focus its light.

Weather vane

Light is visible 16 miles (25 km) away

Lattice mast

3,000-watt electric light bulb

AIR SUPPLIES
Providing supplies to lighthouses by sea has always been difficult and dangerous. A helipad (circular platform) above the lantern makes access by helicopter possible. Landing requires considerable skill, especially in very bad weather.

LUMINOUS LANTERN
A rotating lens assembly surrounds the lamp. The lenses concentrate the light into several narrow beams. A motor moves the lenses around the lamp, so that the beams scan the ocean, producing the characteristic flashes of the lighthouse.

JOBS FOR THE BUOYS
The Lanby – *l*arge *a*utomatic *n*avigational *b*uoy – replaces a lightship. The unmanned buoy has a diameter of 39 ft (12 m) and carries a foghorn and radar beacon. This buoy can be moored in any depth of water up to 300 ft (90 m).

Model of the third Eddystone light, built in 1759

EDDYSTONE LIGHTHOUSE
England's most famous lighthouse warns sailors of the Eddystone Rocks near Plymouth. Storms destroyed the first light and the second burned down. During the fire, its keeper swallowed a lump of molten lead and miraculously lived for 12 days. The third Eddystone was the first modern granite rock lighthouse.

Communications

I require assistance

BY SIGNALING WITH FLAGS, lights, sound, or radio, the crew of a crippled ship can summon help or warn vessels of unseen danger. Emergency communications are so vital that mariners of all nations have agreed on standard distress calls. Radio operators tune their sets to a frequency reserved for emergency signals and broadcast "Mayday." This word is from (venez) *m'aider*, which means "(come) help me" in French. In Morse code the distress signal is "SOS," a set of letters chosen because they are easy to send and because they rarely occur together in a normal message. Modern rescue beacons broadcast automatically, but sailors still learn the traditional distress signals, since their lives may depend on them.

SEMAPHORE SIGNALING
When naval ships were close enough, their crews signaled with hand flags. The British semaphore system indicated letters by the angles of two flags. In American wigwag code, the waving of a single flag communicated the message.

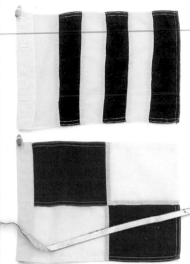

Rocks ahead

READING THE SIGNS
The sailor's nickname for a telescope – "bring-'em-near" – wittily describes what it did for flag signals, making them many times easier to read.

Table of signaling flags

Eyepiece

Morse code sending key

TAPPING OUT THE MESSAGE
By tapping a key such as this, radio operators could broadcast the alphabet in a code of long and short pulses, known as Morse code. When Samuel Morse devised the code in 1837, 50 years before the invention of radio, it was communicated using signaling lamps – a method still widely used at sea.

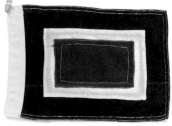

You are steering toward the center of a typhoon

TALKING FLAGS
Flag signaling is an ancient art, but in the 19th century the introduction of a standard code helped mariners make better use of it. The code book, published worldwide, gave the meaning of thousands of flag combinations. To save time, urgent messages use the fewest flags.

Horn produces loud blast of air

Bellows

NOISY BOX
In fog, steamships avoided collisions by blowing their horns or whistles. On sailing ships a hand-powered foghorn blew out a warning loud enough to be heard a mile (1.6 km) away. A handle was wound to gradually fill the bellows with air. The air was then discharged through the horn in a deafening blast.

MECHANICAL SEMAPHORE

A French engineer, Claude Chappé, invented a visual telegraph in 1794. At the top of a tall mast, the position of its adjustable arms represented the letters of the alphabet. Variations of Chappé's telegraph transmitted two or three letters a minute.

Eyepiece

Shutter trigger

ALDIS LAMP

The invention of the electric light made signaling lamps more powerful. Inventor Arthur Aldis perfected the lamp named after him. Its trigger-operated shutter flashed the light more rapidly than a switch.

On/off lamp trigger

Clapper

RINGING OUT A WARNING

In fog a ship's bell gave an audible warning of its position. However, sound is a poor way of sending more detailed signals. Strong wind, for instance, can drown out the sound of a bell. The bell also functioned as a clock during each four-hour watch on board ship. The bell was struck every half hour during the watch.

A VERY GOOD IDEA

A distress rocket or flare is visible even when waves hide the ship that fired it. United States naval officer Edward Very (1847–1910) devised a pistol to fire them high into the sky. Modern rockets do not need a separate firing mechanism.

Pistol opened like an ordinary gun

Body (frame)

WEBLEY & SCOTT LTD
LONDON & BIRMINGHAM

Stock (grip)

Rope for ringing out a warning in fog, or for chiming the time

Cartridge fitted into wide barrel

SIGNALING LAMP

By flashing a light, ships several miles apart can communicate on a clear night. In 1867, British Admiral Philip Colomb suggested using a code of long and short flashes. Colomb's system of flashing signals was soon replaced by Morse code.

WIRELESS COMMUNICATION

The invention of radio in 1895 provided a powerful new way of communicating. Ships were quick to take advantage of "wireless telegraphy," especially after the *Titanic* disaster (pp. 28–29) proved its lifesaving value.

Sailor signals to distant ships in Morse code

Shipwreck survivors

THOSE WHO ESCAPE A SINKING SHIP celebrate their good luck only briefly, for their ordeal is just beginning. The obvious danger they face is drowning, but cold seas can also kill in minutes. Life rafts provide protection against both, but perhaps the cruelest hazard of all is thirst. Seawater is everywhere, but it contains salt, and drinking it makes the body dehydrated. When fresh water runs out, it is better to drink nothing and wait for rain. Thirst may torture survivors, but it will not kill them for two weeks – provided they can avoid the moisture loss caused by sweating. Food is surprisingly unimportant, but shelter is crucial; sunlight consumes vital water and burns and blisters the skin. Suffering these hazards has driven shipwrecked mariners mad, but those who are determined enough to endure them have been rescued after more than four months at sea.

RAFT OF THE CANNIBALS
When the French ship *Medusa* ran aground off Africa's coast in July 1816, passengers and crew huddled aboard a makeshift raft. While it drifted for 12 days, all but 15 died or were killed in fights. Survivors lived off the flesh of the dead. The affair shocked French people even before Théodore Géricault (1791–1824) completed this painting of their ordeal in 1816.

Karluk survivors sewed clothes from animal skins

LIFESAVING RECLINER
Ordinary wooden lifeboats need to be launched by experienced crew – perhaps when a ship is sinking and the passengers are panicking. Deck-seat rafts, by contrast, drift free as the ship sinks, or can simply be thrown into the water. The most basic are little more than large floats, but this deck-seat lifeboat provided a bit more protection to those on board.

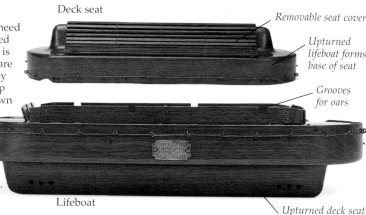

Deck seat

Removable seat cover

Upturned lifeboat forms base of seat

Grooves for oars

Lifeboat

Upturned deck seat forms a lifeboat

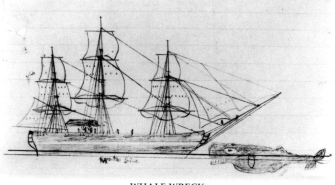

WHALE WRECK
When a whale rammed the *Essex* in the Pacific Ocean in 1820, the crew escaped in rowboats. Some survived for three months, tortured by storms, sharks, and hunger. They ate the bodies of those who died, then killed and ate Owen Coffin, the cabin boy. Herman Melville made the story famous in his 1851 novel *Moby Dick*.

Supplies of food and water

20-30 survivors shared raft

KARLUK SURVIVORS
When Arctic ice trapped his ship, the *Karluk*, in 1913, Canadian explorer Vilhjalmur Stefansson took off with the best dogs and a few crew members. The abandoned crew survived for nearly a year on an Arctic island after pack ice (p. 11) crushed the ship. The *Karluk*'s captain traveled 700 m (1,120 km) to get help, but many crew members died of cold, suicide, and disease before rescuers found them. Stefansson was presumed dead but turned up in 1918, having survived five years in the Arctic.

CHIPCHASE LIFE RAFT
The danger of torpedoes in World War II forced crews to abandon ship quickly. A quick-release mechanism sent the wooden Chipchase raft sliding down its launch ramp into the sea.

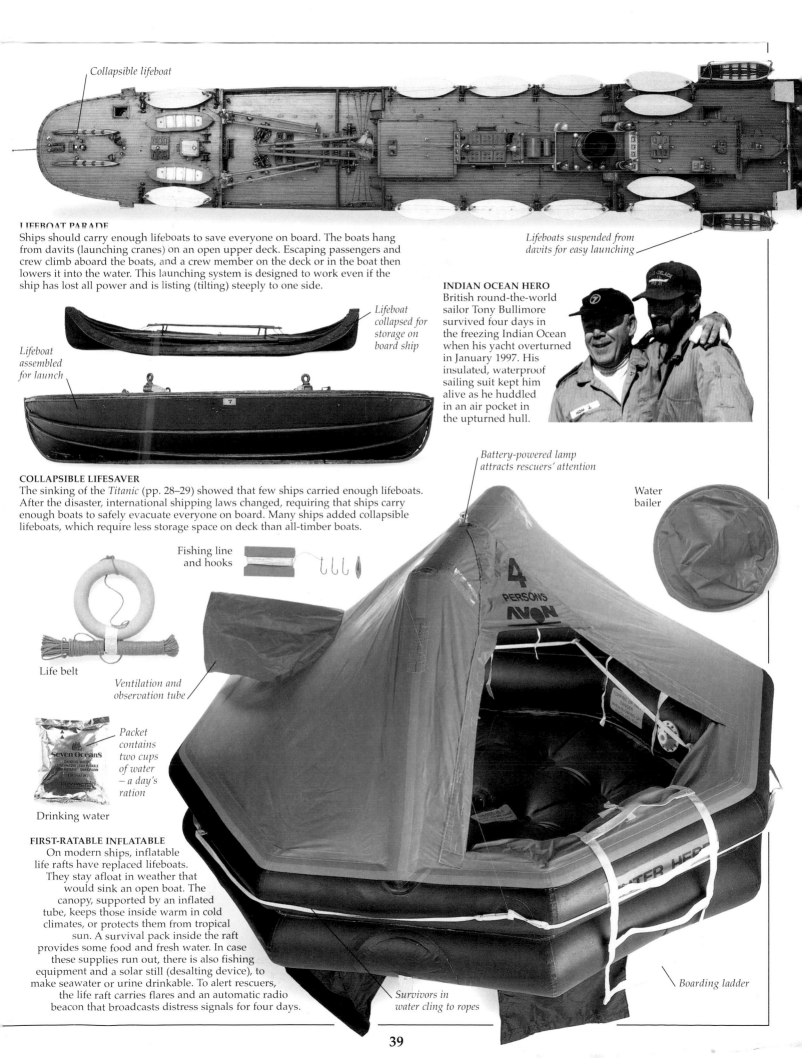

Collapsible lifeboat

Lifeboats suspended from davits for easy launching

LIFEBOAT PARADE

Ships should carry enough lifeboats to save everyone on board. The boats hang from davits (launching cranes) on an open upper deck. Escaping passengers and crew climb aboard the boats, and a crew member on the deck or in the boat then lowers it into the water. This launching system is designed to work even if the ship has lost all power and is listing (tilting) steeply to one side.

Lifeboat collapsed for storage on board ship

Lifeboat assembled for launch

INDIAN OCEAN HERO

British round-the-world sailor Tony Bullimore survived four days in the freezing Indian Ocean when his yacht overturned in January 1997. His insulated, waterproof sailing suit kept him alive as he huddled in an air pocket in the upturned hull.

COLLAPSIBLE LIFESAVER

The sinking of the *Titanic* (pp. 28–29) showed that few ships carried enough lifeboats. After the disaster, international shipping laws changed, requiring that ships carry enough boats to safely evacuate everyone on board. Many ships added collapsible lifeboats, which require less storage space on deck than all-timber boats.

Battery-powered lamp attracts rescuers' attention

Water bailer

Fishing line and hooks

Life belt

Ventilation and observation tube

Packet contains two cups of water – a day's ration

Drinking water

FIRST-RATABLE INFLATABLE

On modern ships, inflatable life rafts have replaced lifeboats. They stay afloat in weather that would sink an open boat. The canopy, supported by an inflated tube, keeps those inside warm in cold climates, or protects them from tropical sun. A survival pack inside the raft provides some food and fresh water. In case these supplies run out, there is also fishing equipment and a solar still (desalting device), to make seawater or urine drinkable. To alert rescuers, the life raft carries flares and an automatic radio beacon that broadcasts distress signals for four days.

Survivors in water cling to ropes

Boarding ladder

Air and sea rescues

WHEN A DISTRESS CALL SUMMONS LIFEBOAT CREWS, they do not waste a second. They jump into waterproof clothes and hurriedly board the rescue boat, for the slightest delay can mean lost lives. The vessel they launch is called a lifeboat, but it has little else in common with survival craft launched from sinking ships. These lifeboats are speedy and unsinkable; they are specially built to search for and rescue mariners in distress. There are many types, from inshore inflatables to large offshore lifeboats that can answer distress calls up to 50 miles (80 km) away. Lifeboats cannot reach more distant emergencies quickly enough, so helicopters respond to those calls.

LIFEBOAT PIONEER
The world's first national lifeboat service began in England in 1824. It was the creation of William Hillary (1771–1847), a lifeboat crewman on the Isle of Man. He founded the Shipwreck Institution, which is now called the Royal National Lifeboat Institution (RNLI).

HORSES FOR COURSES
Lifeboats stationed on flat beaches may be far from the sea at low tide. Before they can launch the boat, the crew must take it to the water. In the past, a team of horses dragged the boat into the surf on a carriage. Now a tractor provides the power.

Horse-drawn lifeboat

Greathead lifeboat

Cork flotation aids

Trailer for launching lifeboat into the water

SAFETY AT SEA
Early lifeboats did not sink in rough seas, but if they capsized, they were difficult to turn the right way up. Self-righting designs, such as this 28-ft (8.5-m) rowboat (left), appeared in the 1850s. Nevertheless, some lifeboat crews preferred traditional boats that were easier to handle and keep upright.

FIRST LIFEBOATS
Seafaring folk have a long tradition of lifesaving using ordinary boats. In the late 18th century, various inventors in Britain and France suggested adding iron keels and extra flotation aids to make these boats more suitable for rescue. This Greathead lifeboat, built in 1790, was among the first of the unsinkable designs.

In small communities where no motorized transport existed, lifeboats often had to be dragged a long distance before and after a rescue

HEAVE-HO!
Coastal communities have a special reason to support the work of lifeboats. Everybody has a relative or a friend in the crew, and many of the rescues pluck local mariners and fishermen from the sea. So when a lifeboat needs to be hauled up the beach, everyone lends a hand.

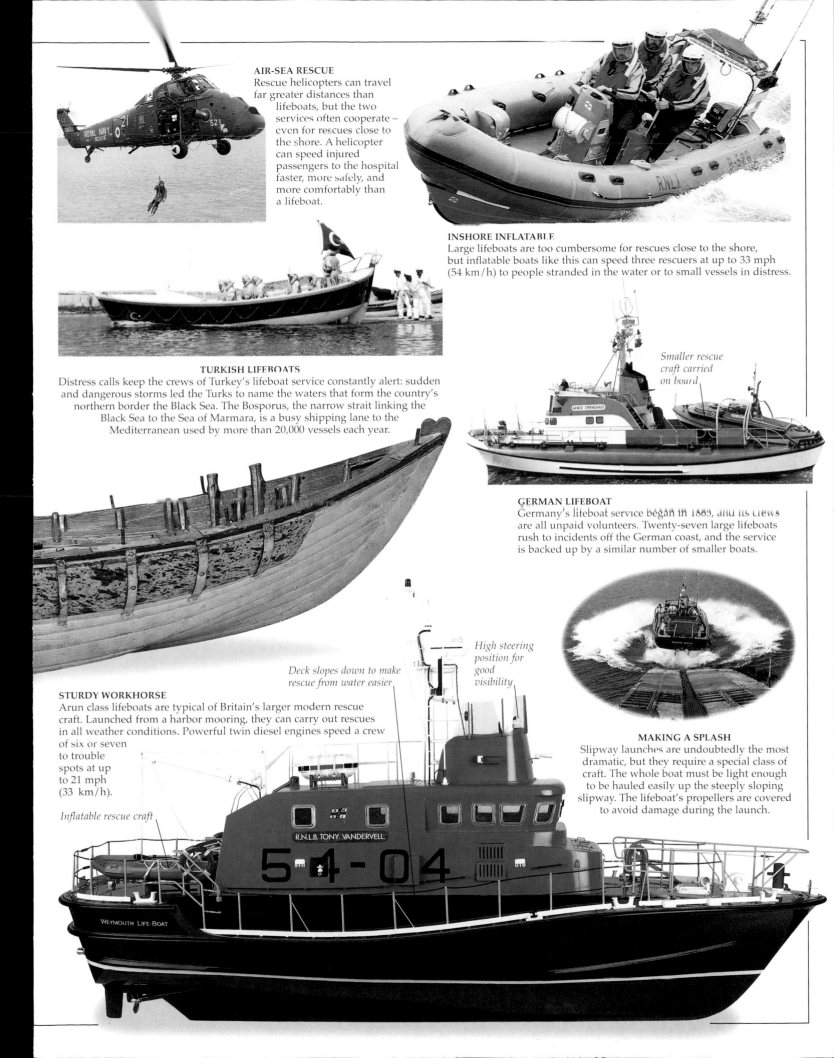

AIR-SEA RESCUE
Rescue helicopters can travel far greater distances than lifeboats, but the two services often cooperate – even for rescues close to the shore. A helicopter can speed injured passengers to the hospital faster, more safely, and more comfortably than a lifeboat.

INSHORE INFLATABLE
Large lifeboats are too cumbersome for rescues close to the shore, but inflatable boats like this can speed three rescuers at up to 33 mph (54 km/h) to people stranded in the water or to small vessels in distress.

TURKISH LIFEBOATS
Distress calls keep the crews of Turkey's lifeboat service constantly alert: sudden and dangerous storms led the Turks to name the waters that form the country's northern border the Black Sea. The Bosporus, the narrow strait linking the Black Sea to the Sea of Marmara, is a busy shipping lane to the Mediterranean used by more than 20,000 vessels each year.

Smaller rescue craft carried on board

GERMAN LIFEBOAT
Germany's lifeboat service began in 1865, and its crews are all unpaid volunteers. Twenty-seven large lifeboats rush to incidents off the German coast, and the service is backed up by a similar number of smaller boats.

STURDY WORKHORSE
Arun class lifeboats are typical of Britain's larger modern rescue craft. Launched from a harbor mooring, they can carry out rescues in all weather conditions. Powerful twin diesel engines speed a crew of six or seven to trouble spots at up to 21 mph (33 km/h).

Inflatable rescue craft

Deck slopes down to make rescue from water easier

High steering position for good visibility

MAKING A SPLASH
Slipway launches are undoubtedly the most dramatic, but they require a special class of craft. The whole boat must be light enough to be hauled easily up the steeply sloping slipway. The lifeboat's propellers are covered to avoid damage during the launch.

R.N.L.B. TONY VANDERVELL

5 4-04

WEYMOUTH LIFE-BOAT

Lifeboat equipment

IN THE BRIDGE, OR WHEELHOUSE, of a modern lifeboat, computers and radio equipment help the crew to speed toward vessels in distress. Automatic navigation systems pinpoint the lifeboat's location with the aid of radio signals from satellites and coastal beacons. A computerized chart plotter shows the surrounding coastline, buoys, and hazards. A sonic depth finder measures water depth. Radio equipment allows the crew to keep in touch with other rescue services and with the vessel in trouble. For the rescue itself, though, equipment has changed little in 50 years. Below are some of the tools and tackle that lifeboats carry, but one important detail is missing—the bravery of the volunteer crew is the most vital equipment of all, for without it every rescue attempt would fail.

PRACTICE MAKES PERFECT
There is no substitute for hands-on rescue experience, but lifeboat crews need first-aid training so they can treat casualties properly. Other courses teach skills in the use of radar and radio equipment.

BOAT HOOK
With the help of a boat hook, rescuers can pull a small crippled vessel alongside the lifeboat or hold on to someone floating in the water.

Rope is fired from this end

SPEEDLINE DEVICE
Pulling the trigger fires a rocket that carries a line of rope a distance of 755 ft (230 m).

Cordage (rope)

HAND-HELD FLARES
Flares that produce a brilliant red flame or a plume of orange smoke are used to catch the attention of other rescuers.

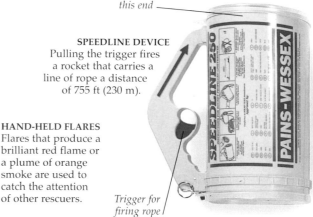

SPEEDLINE 250 — PAINS-WESSEX

Trigger for firing rope

ROPE AND PULLEY
Threading a rope through a block and tackle (pulley) makes a life buoy easier to recover from water.

Block and tackle

Nozzle

FIRE FIGHTING
When going alongside a burning vessel, the crew protects the lifeboat from the flames by dousing it with water from a fire hose. A portable fire extinguisher is used to tackle any small fires on board the lifeboat.

troll FIRST + AID

Fire hose

Portable fire extinguisher

BILGE PUMP
Small enough to carry onto a waterlogged pleasure craft, this hand pump quickly drains the bilges (the lowest part of the hull) so that the boat floats higher in the water.

ANCHOR AND CHAIN
In shallow water, the anchor prevents a lifeboat from drifting, and keeps its bow headed into the waves.

FIRST-AID KIT
People rescued from the sea often need treatment for hypothermia (low body temperature). The crew uses the first-aid kit to stabilize other injuries, such as burns and broken bones, until they can get the victim to a doctor.

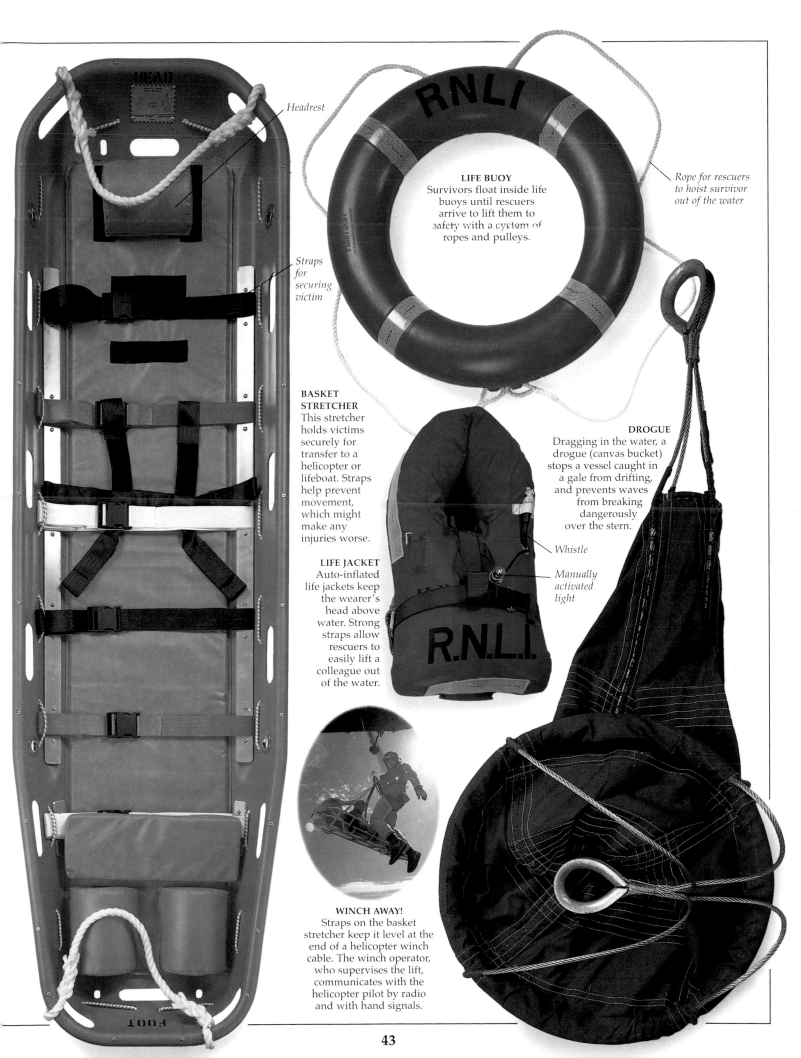

Headrest

Straps for securing victim

LIFE BUOY
Survivors float inside life buoys until rescuers arrive to lift them to safety with a system of ropes and pulleys.

Rope for rescuers to hoist survivor out of the water

BASKET STRETCHER
This stretcher holds victims securely for transfer to a helicopter or lifeboat. Straps help prevent movement, which might make any injuries worse.

DROGUE
Dragging in the water, a drogue (canvas bucket) stops a vessel caught in a gale from drifting, and prevents waves from breaking dangerously over the stern.

LIFE JACKET
Auto-inflated life jackets keep the wearer's head above water. Strong straps allow rescuers to easily lift a colleague out of the water.

Whistle

Manually activated light

R.N.L.I.

WINCH AWAY!
Straps on the basket stretcher keep it level at the end of a helicopter winch cable. The winch operator, who supervises the lift, communicates with the helicopter pilot by radio and with hand signals.

Early diving

VALUABLE CARGOES have always lured swimmers brave enough to dive down to explore sunken wrecks. In ancient Greece divers kept a third of the value of anything that they recovered from wrecks 12 ft (3.7 m) down; their share increased to half for wrecks twice as deep. Since few people can hold their breath for longer than two minutes, as early as the 4th century B.C. divers carried a supply of air trapped inside a barrel or a bell. In 1679, Italian scientist Giovanni Borelli (1608–79) suggested prolonging dives by refreshing the air in the "diving bell" using a simple pump. For the next 250 years divers used pumped-air techniques to reach shipwrecks as deep as 200 ft (60 m).

Metal bands hold the wooden timbers firmly in place

BARREL DIVER
English diver John Lethbridge built one of the first practical diving bells in 1715. Lowered on a rope to wrecks as deep as 30 ft (9 m), it contained enough air for a half-hour's work. Diving for wrecks inside his barrel earned the inventor a fortune.

Simple signals were communicated to the surface by tugging on the rope

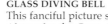

GLASS DIVING BELL
This fanciful picture shows Greek king Alexander the Great (356–323 B.C.) as a diver. His glass diving bell would never have worked; water pressure would have crushed the glass, and the lamps would have burned up all the oxygen.

COMMUNICATIONS BENEATH THE SEA
From about 1900, divers were able to communicate using microphones and small loudspeakers inside their helmets. Wire connected them to a miniature "telephone exchange" on the surface ship. The surface crew could listen to four divers at a time, flipping switches to talk to each of them in turn.

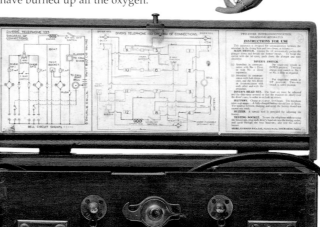

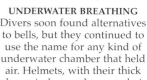

UNDERWATER BREATHING
Divers soon found alternatives to bells, but they continued to use the name for any kind of underwater chamber that held air. Helmets, with their thick glass window and pumped-air supply, enabled divers to make longer, more adventurous dives.

DIVE WEIGHTS
The air in divers' suits and helmets made them buoyant (lighter than water), so they floated. To descend to a wreck, divers strapped heavy lead weights over their suits.

Copper and brass helmet

CLOSED-CIRCUIT DIVING
The air that divers exhale contains carbon dioxide. By absorbing this poisonous gas, a closed circuit diving apparatus, such as this Italian mask from World War II, made the air fit for breathing again.

Pumped-air supply hose

Glass window

Straps attach mask to head

Twin-hose demand valve

Air supply gauge

END OF THE HOSE
The invention of the demand valve (p. 46) freed divers from cumbersome suits. Wearing compressed air cylinders on their backs and a mask, such as this German mask from the 1950s, they no longer had to rely on air pumped from the surface. This self-contained breathing apparatus (p. 46) enabled divers to descend safely to wrecks 165 ft (50 m) underwater.

AIRHEAD
An air hose and a safety line linked a diver wearing a Siebe suit to the surface ship. There, a crew member operated a pump to force air down the tube and into the diver's helmet. The safety line was for raising the diver from the wreck, and for communicating simple signals.

Rubber cuffs

Layer of rubber sandwiched between canvas

SIEBE SUIT
In a heavy suit with a globelike helmet, 19th-century divers could leave their diving bells and explore more freely. German watchmaker Augustus Siebe developed the first completely enclosed suit around 1830. For safety the Siebe helmets were sealed to the diver's waterproof suit. Earlier dive helmets were loose and could fill with water if the diver fell.

Leather boots with lead bases to weigh down the diver

Scuba diving

To SWIM THROUGH A WRECK as free as a fish—this was always the dream of divers exploring the seabed. In 1943, a French naval officer Jacques Yves Cousteau, made the dream a reality. His Aqua-Lung used a novel regulator to control the pressure and flow of air from a cylinder on the diver's back. When the diver breathed in, the regulator opened to allow air to flow to the mouthpiece. The freedom of movement provided by the Aqua-Lung, or scuba (self-contained *underwater breathing apparatus*) diving equipment, led to the discovery and exploration of many new wrecks.

BUOYANCY CONTROL DEVICE
To swim effortlessly at a constant depth, divers wear inflatable jackets called buoyancy control devices (BCDs). Air in the lungs and suit gives divers positive buoyancy—they float. Weights give them negative buoyancy—they sink. By adjusting the amount of air in their BCDs, divers achieve neutral buoyancy—they move neither up nor down.

Air supply tube inflates BCD more quickly than the air from divers' lungs

First stage on tank greatly reduces air pressure

Blowing air into mouthpiece inflates jacket

Distress whistle for use on the surface of the water

Dump valve for manual expulsion of air from the jacket

Reserve air tank

Demand valve on mouthpiece lets air flow when diver inhales

Emergency mouthpiece, or octopus

UNDERWATER BREATHING APPARATUS
Carried on a harness on the diver's back, the underwater breathing apparatus draws air at high pressure from a large tank. Valves on top of the tank and on the mouthpieces reduce air pressure to the correct level for breathing.

Air tank

Compass

Depth gauge

Pressure gauge warns of low air supply

UNDERWATER VISION
Masks may leak underwater, causing blurred vision. They are easily cleared, however, by tilting the head back and exhaling through the nose, thereby purging the mask.

Wave breaker

SNORKEL
Gripped in the mouth, a breathing tube, or snorkel, supplies air to a diver just below the surface of the water. Snorkels are short because water pressure makes breathing through them difficult in depths greater than 14 in (35 cm).

Wet suit

KITCHEN SINK INVENTORS
Jacques Cousteau (above) and an engineer, Emile Gagnan, adapted the control valve from a gas stove to equalize the pressure of the ocean with the pressure of the air breathed in by the diver. The new pressure regulator meant air could now be supplied on demand to a diver carrying a tank of compressed air on his back.

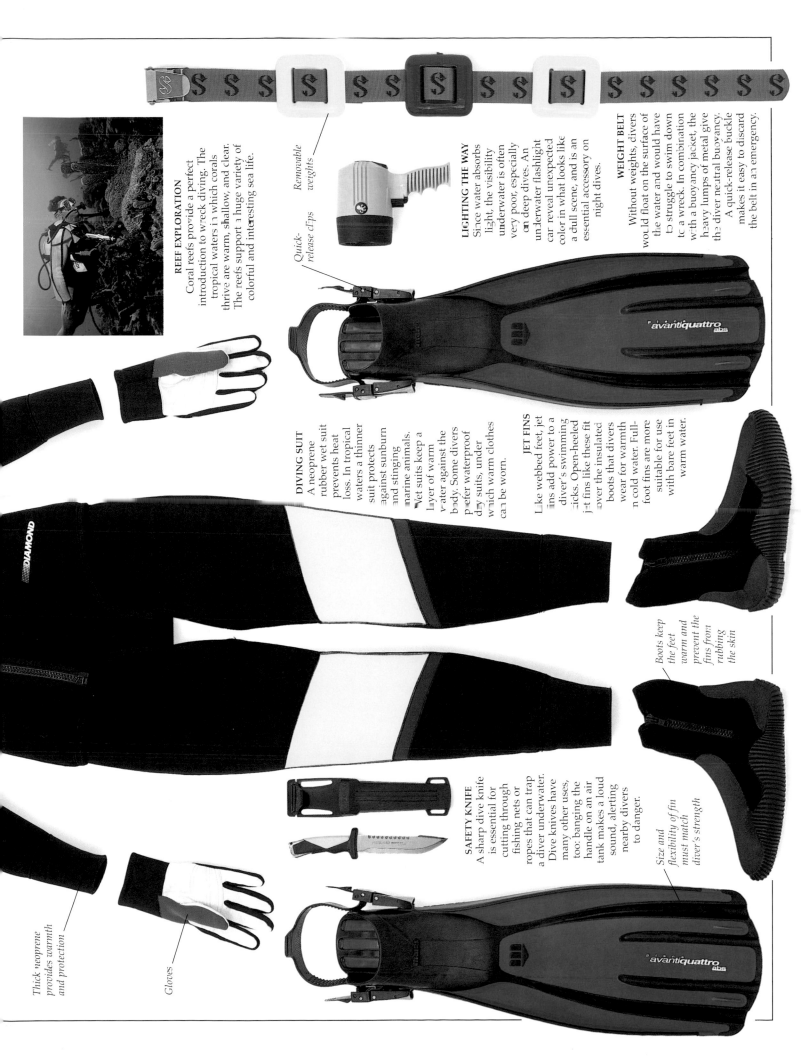

REEF EXPLORATION
Coral reefs provide a perfect introduction to wreck diving. The tropical waters in which corals thrive are warm, shallow, and clear. The reefs support a huge variety of colorful and interesting sea life.

Removable weights

Quick-release clips

LIGHTING THE WAY
Since water absorbs light, the visibility underwater is often very poor, especially on deep dives. An underwater flashlight can reveal unexpected color in what looks like a dull scene, and is an essential accessory on night dives.

WEIGHT BELT
Without weights, divers would float on the surface of the water and would have to struggle to swim down to a wreck. In combination with a buoyancy jacket, the heavy lumps of metal give the diver neutral buoyancy. A quick-release buckle makes it easy to discard the belt in an emergency.

DIVING SUIT
A neoprene rubber wet suit prevents heat loss. In tropical waters a thinner suit protects against sunburn and stinging marine animals. Wet suits keep a layer of warm water against the body. Some divers prefer waterproof dry suits, under which warm clothes can be worn.

JET FINS
Like webbed feet, jet fins add power to a diver's swimming kicks. Open-heeled jet fins like these fit over the insulated boots that divers wear for warmth in cold water. Full-foot fins are more suitable for use with bare feet in warm water.

Boots keep the feet warm and prevent the fins from rubbing the skin

SAFETY KNIFE
A sharp dive knife is essential for cutting through fishing nets or ropes that can trap a diver underwater. Dive knives have many other uses, too: banging the handle on an air tank makes a loud sound, alerting nearby divers to danger.

Size and flexibility of fin must match diver's strength

Thick neoprene provides warmth and protection

Gloves

Deep-sea exploration

SINKING BELOW THE WAVES, a wrecked ship slips out of sight – and perhaps out of reach. The ocean filters out the sun's light and heat, leaving a cold, dark world. The deeper a wreck sinks, the more water presses down on it from above. Deep wreck sites are dangerous places for divers because the water pressure dissolves nitrogen gas in a diver's blood, causing narcosis – a kind of drunkenness. Divers must surface slowly, or risk developing decompression sickness (the bends) as the nitrogen forms bubbles in the veins. A wreck deeper than 330 ft (100 m) is beyond the reach of scuba divers, but divers in rigid suits can descend to 2,000 ft (600 m), and submarines can reach even deeper wrecks.

PERESS SUIT
Inside a rigid atmospheric diving suit (ADS), the diver breathes air at atmospheric (normal) pressure and can surface without having to enter a decompression chamber (right). In 1930, Joseph Peress developed a successful ADS. Flexible joints in the arms and legs enabled the diver to move at a depth of 1,000 ft (300 m).

Suit was nicknamed "Jim" for Jim Jarrett, who tested the prototype

Ports on suit gave limited vision

Diver operated claws from inside the suit

DIVERS' DEN
To avoid the bends, divers enter a decompression chamber upon surfacing from deep dives. The chamber is filled with high-pressure air. As the pressure drops, excess nitrogen passes from the blood into the lungs, and is then exhaled safely.

DEEP WRECK
Using even the most sophisticated equipment, divers may have only a few minutes to investigate a deep wreck before their blood absorbs dangerous amounts of nitrogen.

ASHERAH SUBMERSIBLE
Techniques and equipment developed for deep dives can also be valuable aids in shallower water. In 1964, the University of Pennsylvania launched the first-ever submersible, *Asherah* – a submarine specially customized for underwater archaeology. It was first used to survey a wreck at Yassi Ada, Turkey, in water 140 ft (42 m) deep. Led by George Bass, the first land archaeologist to study an underwater wreck, the team of two was able to map the site rapidly.

Frames form a ruled grid through which photographs of the wreck can be taken, and later pieced together to give an overall picture of the site

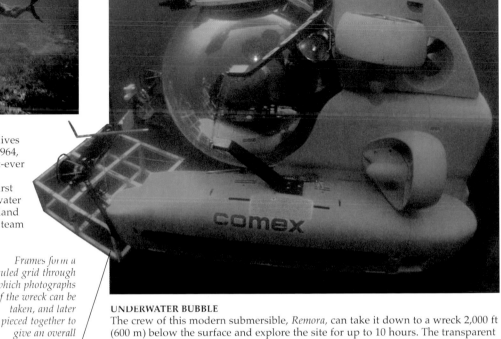

UNDERWATER BUBBLE
The crew of this modern submersible, *Remora*, can take it down to a wreck 2,000 ft (600 m) below the surface and explore the site for up to 10 hours. The transparent bubble "cab" provides spectacular all-around views for the pilot and observer. With the aid of thrusters (propellers), *Remora* is able to hover like a helicopter.

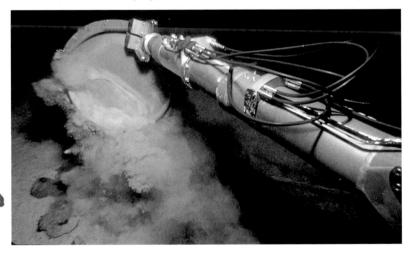

ARMS ACROSS THE OCEAN
Inside a submersible, the crew cannot reach out and touch the objects they see, as a free-swimming diver can. However, a jointed arm controlled from inside the vessel allows the crew to grip and retrieve loose artifacts from the wreck.

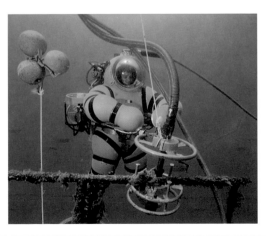

NEWT SUIT
ADS equipment is tiring for the operator inside, because at great depths the water pressure makes the suit stiffen. The fluid-filled joints of the Drager Newt Suit (left) reduce the problem, allowing divers roughly three quarters of normal mobility. Despite this improvement, the suits are still cumbersome, but the addition of electric thrusters makes them easier to maneuver. Newt suits can reach wrecks 1,000 ft (300 m) down.

PLOTTING ARTIFACTS
The first step of any archaeological investigation of a shipwreck is a pre-disturbance survey. Divers make a grid, dividing the site exactly into squares using poles and wires. They can then record in which square each artifact lies, and measure its position within the square – including its depth below the grid. Finally, using photographs or sketches, they collect enough data to draw a map of the site.

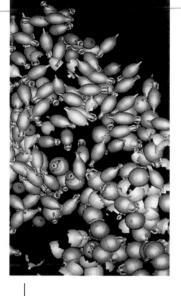

RAISING THE CARGO
To study a wreck site in detail, archaeologists need to first remove the mud or silt that covers its surface. They work slowly and carefully, recording every significant detail. Gentle fanning with the hand is often enough to remove soft silt. Heavier materials require powerful tools such as a propeller wash – a water jet that blows away mud. Once the divers have recorded finds, they raise them with the help of an airlift – a buoyant, air-filled bag.

Wreck location and recovery

ONE OF THE MOST EFFECTIVE ways to locate a wreck is to ask fishermen where their nets get snagged! A more systematic approach, however, is to search dusty marine archives for the ship's last known position. If this reveals roughly where the wreck sank, technology can narrow the search. Sonar (sound navigation ranging) surveys the contours of a wreck. Side-scan sonar (below) surveys large areas of the seabed using sound waves to produce a clearly definable "shadow" photograph. Magnetometers create magnetic maps of the seabed. These show the location of metal objects such as cannons – even if deep mud covers them. Marine archaeologists plan their dives by using the charts that these instruments provide. Raising the wreck and cargo is obviously part of the task ahead. It is just as important, however, to record where each object rested. So before surfacing with their finds, divers spend much of their time underwater measuring, mapping, sketching, and taking photographs.

SIDEWAYS VIEW
Side-scan sonar mapping gives either a "broad view" of a wreck or a "close look." It reveals objects roughly 1/400th the size of the scan width, so to reveal an object as small as an amphora, the scan must be no wider than 400 amphorae.

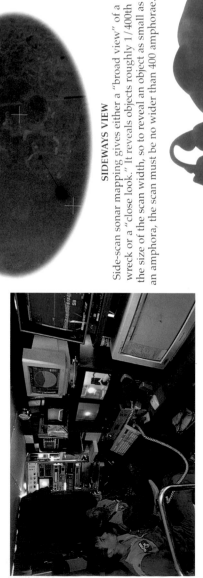

STUDYING THE WRECK SITE
Sometimes scientists have their first view of the wreck without even having to get their feet wet. Cables carry signals from remote sensing devices, like sonar, up to a control room on the survey ship, where they appear on computer monitors or plotters.

Large anchor provides a clear marker for this wreck site

Diver surveys a wreck before beginning to sketch the site

SEABED SURVEY

Pulled along underwater at the end of a 1,320-ft (400-m) cable, the cigar-shaped sonar "towfish" maps the seabed using "pings" of sound waves. Sensors pick up echoes of the pulses, and the towfish transmits them up a cable to the survey vessel for viewing and interpretation.

Life on board ship

"ABANDON SHIP!" When seafarers hear these dreaded words, they drop whatever they are doing and rush for their lives. There is rarely time to gather property—and rescue boats have no room for luggage. So countless personal possessions and everyday objects sink with the wreck. When carefully raised and documented, these items can provide a wealth of information. Most objects are ordinary, and nobody would call them sunken treasure, but to the marine archaeologist they can be worth more than a cargo of gold. The abandoned possessions of the crew give a vivid picture of what life was like on board a ship. Tools and equipment may provide clues to the identity and date of a wreck. The location of these implements can also help archaeologists to assemble—jigsaw fashion— parts of a wreck that have been broken up by strong ocean currents.

COOKING UP A STORM
During a storm, the threat of a fire on board was an unnecessary additional hazard. Therefore, a sailing ship's cook extinguished the stove. The crew ate cold food until the weather improved.

Measure held just enough powder to fire a cannon once

EXPLOSIVE MEASURES
Warships had a magazine (storeroom) where gunpowder was measured out into silk bags. The discovery of a gunpowder measure, such as this one from the British flagship *Ramillies*, may pinpoint the location of the magazine.

GUN CARRIAGE
Wooden gun carriages did not float away from wrecks, because the cannons they supported weighed them down. This carriage held a signaling gun about 4 ft (1.2 m) long.

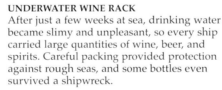

UNDERWATER WINE RACK
After just a few weeks at sea, drinking water became slimy and unpleasant, so every ship carried large quantities of wine, beer, and spirits. Careful packing provided protection against rough seas, and some bottles even survived a shipwreck.

PHARMACIST'S STOCK
Medical treatment was primitive in the age of sailing, and more sailors died of disease than of drowning. The drugs that these bottles once contained were probably reserved for the officers. The ship that carried them, the *Earl of Abergavenny*, sank after running aground in February 1805.

SHIP SNIPPERS
Seawater often corrodes iron and steel objects, but a few may escape destruction, especially where the water lacks oxygen. These scissors, recovered from a ship that sank more than two centuries ago, are still able to cut paper and cloth.

ONE-SHOT WONDER
Flintlock pistols needed to be reloaded after each shot. In hand-to-hand fighting, sailors fired once and then used the pistols as clubs. Two and a half centuries underwater have corroded the barrel of this pistol.

Wood frame is still intact after 250 years in the sea

Bristles have rotted

CRAMPED QUARTERS
Naval seamen shared their meals in messes– groups small enough to sit around a table positioned between the guns. Conditions were cramped, and there was barely enough space for each sailor to store a change of clothes and a few personal items. Officers had more space for their possessions.

RUSH TO BRUSH
Brushing teeth was often a bloody business for sailors: bleeding gums were a symptom of scurvy, caused by bad diet. The British navy began issuing citrus fruits to cure the disease 10 years before the ship carrying these wooden brushes sank in 1805.

HARMONICA RESTORED
Music was not just for entertainment on ships: its regular beats and rhythms helped sailors to pull together on ropes and winches. Raised from the seabed and carefully cleaned in acid (p. 56), these century-old harmonicas still play a sea shanty in tune.

CUTLERY MASS
Rust can transform wreck artifacts into an iron-hard mass. This lump of ensnared cutlery is from the *Aurania*, a liner that worked as a British troopship during World War I. Torpedoes sank the *Aurania* off the Irish coast in 1918.

Silver-plated fork

Brass stopper

Silver-plated spoon

Loop held hemp rope

SOUNDING WEIGHT
In shallow seas, sailors used "lead and lines" to measure the depth of water (sound) under the ship. This lead sounding weight would have been tied to a long rope and hurled overboard. The line went slack when the lead reached the bottom of the sea, and distinctive pieces of leather and cloth tied to the line at intervals indicated the depth. The sailor performing this vital task was the first to know if the ship was about to run aground.

Knife handles

Lost cargoes

IN BUNDLES AND BALES, barrels and boxes, cargo filled the holds of merchant ships. Its weight was essential to keeping the ship upright during a voyage. In a wreck, however, a heavy cargo dragged the ship down. Bringing a cargo to the surface is called salvage. It is worthwhile only if the cargo is valuable and seawater has not harmed it. If a wreck can be identified, old documents can reveal in minute detail the contents of the hold. Therefore, divers often know exactly what they are looking for—even where to find it. They do not always keep everything they bring to the surface, though. Salvage divers must pay the rightful owner a proportion of the value of everything recovered. Even if the wreck has rotted on the seabed for centuries, its cargo still belongs to someone.

COIN CACHE
Piled inside the remains of the hold or scattered by the tides, coins are among the most common finds at wreck sites. Many ships carried currency, and the metals from which coins are made do not corrode.

Spanish and American coins

Notes virtually unharmed after submersion in seawater

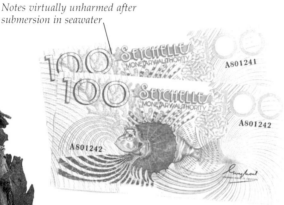

VANISHING BANK NOTES
Wrecked in 1979, the *Aeolian Sky* carried a fortune in Seychelles bank notes. By the time inspection divers reached the wreck, most of the money had been looted. The country's bank canceled the issue, so these notes are now worthless.

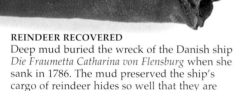

REINDEER RECOVERED
Deep mud buried the wreck of the Danish ship *Die Fraumetta Catharina von Flensburg* when she sank in 1786. The mud preserved the ship's cargo of reindeer hides so well that they are still supple enough to make into clothing.

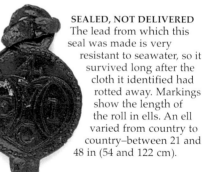

SEALED, NOT DELIVERED
The lead from which this seal was made is very resistant to seawater, so it survived long after the cloth it identified had rotted away. Markings show the length of the roll in ells. An ell varied from country to country–between 21 and 48 in (54 and 122 cm).

COPPER CARGO
Heavy cargo, such as these copper ingots, was stowed very low in the hold to help stabilize the ship. Cast specially for the coppersmiths who worked in the bazaars of India, these ingots sank with the *Earl of Abergavenny* in 1805.

CASH ON THE MOVE
When the SS *Camberwell* struck a floating mine and sank in 1917, India was still a British colony, and its bank notes were printed in England. These 10-rupee notes were part of the ship's general cargo.

READY TO SAIL
Loading, or lading, a ship to make it ready for a voyage was a skilled task, for a cargo that shifted could cause a wreck. Seamen were superstitious about lading. Many believed that a voyage would be successful only if the ship tilted to the port side, or left, as the cargo was loaded.

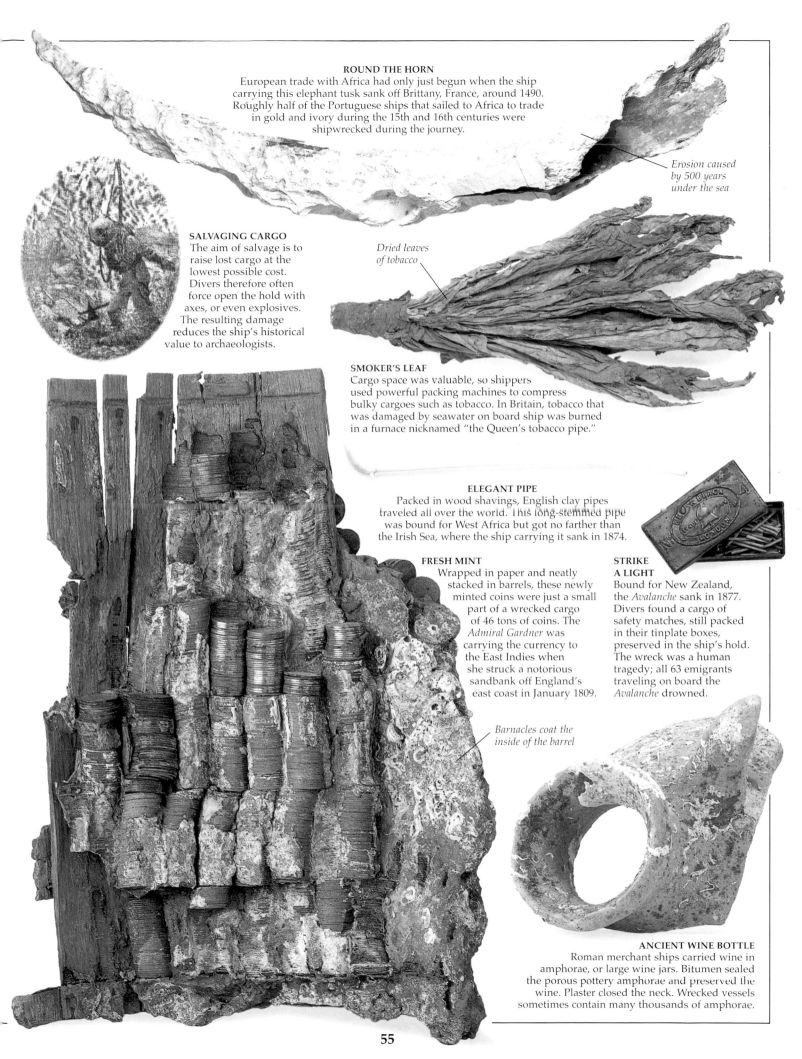

ROUND THE HORN
European trade with Africa had only just begun when the ship carrying this elephant tusk sank off Brittany, France, around 1490. Roughly half of the Portuguese ships that sailed to Africa to trade in gold and ivory during the 15th and 16th centuries were shipwrecked during the journey.

Erosion caused by 500 years under the sea

SALVAGING CARGO
The aim of salvage is to raise lost cargo at the lowest possible cost. Divers therefore often force open the hold with axes, or even explosives. The resulting damage reduces the ship's historical value to archaeologists.

Dried leaves of tobacco

SMOKER'S LEAF
Cargo space was valuable, so shippers used powerful packing machines to compress bulky cargoes such as tobacco. In Britain, tobacco that was damaged by seawater on board ship was burned in a furnace nicknamed "the Queen's tobacco pipe."

ELEGANT PIPE
Packed in wood shavings, English clay pipes traveled all over the world. This long-stemmed pipe was bound for West Africa but got no farther than the Irish Sea, where the ship carrying it sank in 1874.

FRESH MINT
Wrapped in paper and neatly stacked in barrels, these newly minted coins were just a small part of a wrecked cargo of 46 tons of coins. The *Admiral Gardner* was carrying the currency to the East Indies when she struck a notorious sandbank off England's east coast in January 1809.

STRIKE A LIGHT
Bound for New Zealand, the *Avalanche* sank in 1877. Divers found a cargo of safety matches, still packed in their tinplate boxes, preserved in the ship's hold. The wreck was a human tragedy; all 63 emigrants traveling on board the *Avalanche* drowned.

Barnacles coat the inside of the barrel

ANCIENT WINE BOTTLE
Roman merchant ships carried wine in amphorae, or large wine jars. Bitumen sealed the porous pottery amphorae and preserved the wine. Plaster closed the neck. Wrecked vessels sometimes contain many thousands of amphorae.

Reconstruction and preservation

WHEN DIVERS HAVE FINISHED measuring and taking photographs of a wreck, they attempt to raise it from the ocean floor (pp. 50–51). Study and conservation begins on dry land. Objects made of hard materials such as stone may need only washing. Most, however, require further treatment. Timbers shrink, and iron objects such as cannons sometimes corrode so quickly in air that they actually fizz and heat up. Museum conservators have developed treatments to stop or reverse this decay. Their most important task is to protect the finds for historians to study, but they also need to show them to the public. It is not always easy to do both. Objects that fascinate scholars may look like dull lumps of wood to museum visitors, and the public display of a fragile treasure for one year can do more damage than a century spent under the sea.

CORAL BOTTLE
The tiny shells of dead sea creatures can add to the beauty of wreck artefacts. However, cleaning may mean destroying the beautiful lace-like coral growing on this bottle.

MUSICAL MOUTHFUL
Rust spreading from submerged iron objects cements everything nearby into a concretion, or shapeless lump. Conservators use chisels to chip off the worst deposits. Electrolysis – passing electricity through metal objects in a chemical bath – slows further corrosion and softens concretions, making them easier to remove.

Cleaned harmonica

Harmonicas in concretion

BARNACLE BOWL
Though its hard glaze protects porcelain against damage, marine creatures often make their homes on crockery in wrecked cargoes. Here their abandoned shells coat a bowl from the Nanking cargo recovered from the Dutch East Indiaman *Geldermalsen,* which sank in 1752.

CLEANING UP
Scraping barnacles off porcelain would scratch its glaze. Rather than risk this, conservators soak the crockery in a diluted acid solution. The acid dissolves some of the crust and softens the remainder so that it washes off without risk of damage.

MEASURING UP

The measurement and study of artifacts raised from a wreck helps to establish the ship's age and purpose. The shape and size of amphorae (ancient jars), for example, can indicate roughly where they came from. By comparing the maker's stamp with a list compiled from thousands of other examples, it is even possible to identify the workshop that made a newly discovered jar.

THE BIG CLEANUP

Compared to the condition of many other wrecks, archaeologists raised the *Vasa* (pp. 26-27) in what could relatively be considered one piece, but they still faced an enormous task. Eleven scientists worked for five months just to clear and clean the hull, which was made from 14,000 pieces. In all, they documented 25,000 objects found in and around the wreck. Reconstruction of the ship took nearly 20 years.

PICK UP THE PIECES

Before archaeologists could re-create this beautiful jug, they had to document exactly where each piece of pottery lay on the seabed. The distribution of the fragments can reveal vital clues as to whether the pot broke before or after the wreck – and thus, perhaps, help explain how the ship sank.

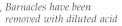
Barnacles have been removed with diluted acid

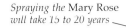
Spraying the Mary Rose *will take 15 to 20 years*

LET US SPRAY

If wood saturated with seawater dries, it shrinks and twists. To prevent this, conservators treat the timbers with a waxy chemical called polyethylene glycol (PEG). Small objects can be soaked in baths, but the only way to treat a whole wreck is to spray it with PEG over a period of several years.

RE-ERECTED WRECK

Tides and currents on the seabed can quickly spread a ship's timbers over a wide area. So once the wood has been stabilized with PEG, conservators attempt to reassemble the pieces of the hull like a giant jigsaw puzzle.

PRESERVATION

Though the crockery now looks perfect, seawater that has penetrated the glaze could crystallize, cracking the plate. Conservators prevent this by soaking the porcelain in a diluted salt solution, gradually reducing the salt concentration over a period of months.

The art of shipwrecks

SHIPWRECKS HAVE ALWAYS fascinated writers, painters, and dramatists, but the very first shipwreck yarns were myths. These traditional stories often featured gods and heroes. Through myths, people in ancient times tried to explain and understand natural forces that governed their lives. In later ages, shipwreck stories enthralled people because they were a terrifying, yet common, experience. Ships were the fastest way to travel, and ocean voyages were more dangerous than they are today. It is not hard to see why shipwrecks still capture the imagination of modern storytellers. Sea voyages bring together people of different characters and backgrounds. The wreck is a dramatic climax. Survival on a raft or island brings out the best – and worst – in everybody, and a rescue always provides a happy ending.

NOAH'S ARK
In the Bible God tells Noah of his plan to flood the earth to cleanse it of evil. Noah builds a ship, the Ark, to save his family and the world's wildlife. After 40 days and nights of heavy rain, the Ark finally runs aground on Mount Ararat, Turkey.

JONAH AND THE WHALE
A Bible book named after Jonah describes his ordeal on a storm-tossed ship in the Mediterranean. Fearing that they will be wrecked, the crew draws lots to see who should be blamed for the squall. When Jonah loses, they throw him overboard, and a "great fish" (believed to have been a whale) swallows the unfortunate mariner.

ROBINSON CRUSOE
Shipwrecked on a desolate island, Robinson Crusoe suffers terrible hardships, ranging from loneliness to cannibal attacks. English author Daniel Defoe (1660–1731) invented the shipwreck featured in his novel, but based Crusoe on Alexander Selkirk (1676–1721), a Scottish sailor who argued with the captain of his ship and asked to be put ashore on a Pacific island.

WHISKY GALORE
When the *Politician* ran aground between the Scottish islands of Eriskay and South Uist in 1941, local people were eager to help unload its cargo—cases of whisky. In *Whisky Galore*, British novelist Compton Mackenzie (1883–1972) turned the consequences of the wreck into hilarious fiction in 1947. A film followed in 1948.

Robinson Crusoe novel

CUTTHROAT ISLAND

Sinking ships do not always make good films. In *Cutthroat Island* (1995), explosions destroy a pirate ship. Critics hated the film, scorning the "dumb storyline" and the bad acting of the hero, played by Geena Davis, the director's wife.

ULYSSES AND THE SIRENS

In his epic poem the *Odyssey*, 9th-century B.C. Greek writer Homer tells the myth of Ulysses, who narrowly escapes shipwreck when he sails past the island home of the sirens. Half woman, half bird, these creatures lure passing mariners onto the rocky island with their sweet songs. Ulysses protects his crew by blocking their ears with wax. The crew then ties him to the mast – but leaves his ears unblocked – so that he can enjoy the sirens' calls.

20,000 LEAGUES UNDER THE SEA

French novelist Jules Verne (1828–1905) conjures up a fantastic underwater world of divers and submarines in his book *20,000 Leagues Under the Sea* (a league is equal to 2.15 miles, or 4 km) written in 1870. Verne's descriptions of diving equipment were incredibly accurate predictions of innovations to come.

ST. NICHOLAS

According to Christian legends, St. Nicholas saved the lives of his shipmates when storms threatened to wreck their little sailing boat off the coast of Turkey. This miracle made him the patron saint of sailors in danger. Also known as Santa Claus, Nicholas was in reality probably a 4th-century bishop of Myra, Turkey.

said she; "I know that I shall love the world up there, and all the people who live in it."

At last she reached her fifteenth year. "Well, now, you are grown up," said the old dowager, her grandmother; "so you must let me adorn you like your other sisters:" and she placed a wreath of white lilies in her hair, and every flower leaf was half a pearl. Then the old lady ordered eight great oysters to attach themselves to the tail of the princess to show her high rank.

"But they hurt me so!" said the little mermaid.

"Pride must suffer pain," replied the old lady. Oh, how gladly she would have shaken off all this grandeur, and laid aside the heavy wreath! The red flowers in her own garden would have suited her much better; but she could not help herself: so she said, "Farewell," and rose as lightly as a bubble to the surface of the water. The sun had just set as she raised her head above the waves; but the clouds were tinted with crimson and gold, and through the glimmering twilight beamed the evening star in all its beauty. The sea was calm, and the air mild and fresh. A large ship, with three masts, lay becalmed on the water, with only one sail set; for not a breeze stirred, and the sailors sat idle on deck or amongst the rigging. There was music and song on board; and, as darkness came on, a hundred coloured lanterns were lighted, as if the flags of all nations waved in the air. The little mermaid swam close to the cabin windows; and now and then, as the waves lifted her up, she could look in through clear glass window-panes, and see a number of well-dressed people within. Among them was a young prince, the most beautiful of all, with large black eyes; he was sixteen years of age, and his birthday was being kept with much rejoicing. The sailors were dancing on deck, but when the prince came out of the cabin, more than a hundred rockets rose in the air, making it as bright as day. The little mermaid was so startled that she dived under water: and when she again stretched out her head, it appeared as if all the stars of heaven were falling around her—she had never seen such fireworks before. Great suns spurted fire about, splendid fire-flies flew into the blue air, and everything was reflected in

"She rose as lightly as a bubble to the surface of the water."—p. 69.

THE CRUEL SEA

In the 1953 British film *The Cruel Sea*, a small group of sailors struggle to survive together on a raft after a submarine sinks their ship. The film's realistic view of World War II (1939–45) heroism made it hugely popular.

THE LITTLE MERMAID

When a terrifying storm wrecks a ship in this charming fairy story, the little mermaid of the title rescues a handsome prince from drowning beneath the ocean waves. To join him on land she swaps her beautiful voice for a pair of human legs. The story was one of many that the Danish author Hans Christian Andersen (1805–75) wrote.

Index

Acknowledgments

Dorling Kindersley would like to thank:
Georgette Purches and Gill Mace of the RNLI, for their invaluable assistance; Charlestown Shipwreck and Heritage Centre, Richard and Bridget Larn; Ocean Leisure, London; Martin Dean and Steve Liscoe at the Archaeological Diving Unit, St Andrews; Jim Pulack at the Institute of Nautical Archaeology, Texas; the Vasa Museum, Stockholm; Simon Stevens, Gloria Clifton, and Barbara Tomlinson of the National Maritime Museum, London; Alan Hills at the British Museum; Darren Troughton, Diane Clouting, Julie Ferris, Carey Scott, Nicki Waine, and Nicola Studdart for editorial and design assistance.

Endpapers: Anna Martin

Index: Chris Bernstein

Picture credits
The publisher would like to thank the following for their kind permission to reproduce the photographs:

(t = top, b = bottom/below, c = center, m = middle, l = left, r = right)

Archaeological Diving Unit, St. Andrew's University: 9br.
Bridgeman Art Library, London/New York: 8cl, 11tr, 15tl, 15cr, 22tr, 22cl, 58tr, 59tl.
Jean Loup Charmet: 34c.
Christie's Images: 16br, 17tl, 17b.
Bruce Coleman: 9tr, 10tr.
Mary Evans Picture Library: 9bl, 14cl, 16tl, 20bl, 28tl, 29tc, 32cl, 36tr, 37tl, 38tl, 59tr.
E.T. Archive: 17tr, 17cr.
Sonia Halliday: 58cl, 59cl.
Robert Harding Picture Library: 10c.
Hulton-Getty: 24tr, 37bc, 44cl.
Ronald Grant Archive: 58bl.

Susan and Michael Katzev: I.N.A. 12bl, 12c.
Image Select: 45bl.
I.N.A. (Institute of Nautical Archaeology), Texas: 13tl, 13tr, 13cl, 13cr, 13bl, 13br; National Geographic/Mr. Bates Littlehales 49tl, 50br.
Kobal Collection: 59bl.
Mary Rose Preservation Trust: 18c, 18b, 19tr, 19c, 57br.
Mansell Collection: 44cr, 55tl.
Nantucket Historical Association: 38c.
National Geographic Image Collection: Edward Kim 16bl, 16c, 16cr; Emory Kristof 24bl, 24–25bc; Richard Schlecht 25tr; Hamilton Scourge Foundation 25br.
National Maritime Museum, London: 14c, 15tr, 21tl, 21br, 22–23bc; R.M.S. Titanic, Inc. 28–29bc, 32c, 32b, 33tl, 33tc, 33c, 36bc, 53tc; Bjorn Landstrom /Vasa Museum 26tr.
Pepys Library, Magdelene

College, Cambridge: 18tr.
Planet Earth Pictures: 46cl.
Popperphoto: 9tl; Portsmouth City Council Museums and Record Service 14bl; R.A.F. Culdrose 35cl.
Rex Features: 9tc, 10bl, 19tl, 33tr, 39cr, 43bc, 47tr, 52c, 56cr, 59tc.
R.N.L.I.: 34cl, 40c, 41tr, 41c, 41cr, 42tl.
Alexis Rosenfeld: 48–49b, 49tr, 49br, 50bl, 50tr, 50trc, 50c, 57tl.
Science Photo Library: 11bl; Klein Associates 25tl, 30tr, 30bl, 31tl, 31tr, 31bc.
Frank Spooner: 30–31c; Gamma 31cr, 31br, 49cr.
Sygma: 29tl, 29tc, 29ct, 29c, 29cr, 30cl.
Telegraph Colour Library: 33br, 41tl, 50–51.
Ulster Museum, Belfast: 22c, 22bl, 23tl, 23tc, 23tr.
Vasa Museum, Stockholm: 26c, 26cl, 26bl, 26–27b, 27tl, 27tr, 27c, 27br, 57c.
Weidenfeld and Nicolson Archives: 38bl.
Zefa: 10cl, 10cr, 33cr, 35c.

SUBJECTS

HISTORY

AFRICA

ANCIENT CHINA

ARMS & ARMOR

BATTLE

CASTLE

COWBOY

EXPLORER

KNIGHT

MEDIEVAL LIFE

MYTHOLOGY

NORTH AMERICAN INDIAN

PIRATE

PRESIDENTS

RUSSIA

SHIPWRECK

TITANIC

VIKING

WITCHES & MAGIC-MAKERS

ANCIENT WORLDS

ANCIENT EGYPT

ANCIENT GREECE

ANCIENT ROME

AZTEC, INCA & MAYA

BIBLE LANDS

MUMMY

PYRAMID

THE BEGINNINGS OF LIFE

ARCHEOLOGY

DINOSAUR

EARLY HUMANS

PREHISTORIC LIFE

THE ARTS

BOOK

COSTUME

DANCE

FILM

MUSIC

TECHNOLOGY

BOAT

CAR

FLYING MACHINE

FUTURE

INVENTION

SPACE EXPLORATION

TRAIN

PAINTING

GOYA

IMPRESSIONISM

LEONARDO & HIS TIMES

MANET

MONET

PERSPECTIVE

RENAISSANCE

VAN GOGH

WATERCOLOR

SCIENCE

ASTRONOMY

CHEMISTRY

EARTH

ECOLOGY

ELECTRICITY

ELECTRONICS

ENERGY

EVOLUTION

FORCE & MOTION

HUMAN BODY

LIFE

LIGHT

MATTER

MEDICINE

SKELETON

TECHNOLOGY

TIME & SPACE

SPORT

BASEBALL

FOOTBALL

OLYMPICS

SOCCER

SPORTS

ANIMALS

AMPHIBIAN

BIRD

BUTTERFLY & MOTH

CAT

DOG

EAGLE &
BIRDS OF PREY

ELEPHANT

FISH

GORILLA,
MONKEY & APE

HORSE

INSECT

MAMMAL

REPTILE

SHARK

WHALE

HABITATS

ARCTIC & ANTARCTIC

DESERT

JUNGLE

OCEAN

POND & RIVER

SEASHORE

THE EARTH

CRYSTAL & GEM

FOSSIL

HURRICANE &
TORNADO

PLANT

ROCKS & MINERALS

SHELL

TREE

VOLCANO &
EARTHQUAKE

WEATHER

THE WORLD AROUND US

BUILDING

CRIME & DETECTION

FARM

FLAG

MEDIA &
COMMUNICATIONS

MONEY

RELIGION

SPY

Future updates and editions will be available online at www.dk.com

A–Z

DK EYEWITNESS BOOKS

1–110

Future updates and editions will be available online at www.dk.com

1 BIRD

2 ROCKS & MINERALS

3 SKELETON

4 ARMS & ARMOR

5 TREE

6 POND & RIVER

7 BUTTERFLY & MOTH

8 SPORTS

9 SHELL

10 EARLY HUMANS

11 MAMMAL

12 MUSIC

13 DINOSAUR

14 PLANT

15 SEASHORE

16 FLAG

17 INSECT

18 MONEY

19 FOSSIL

20 FISH

21 CAR

22 FLYING MACHINE

23 ANCIENT EGYPT

24 ANCIENT ROME

25 CRYSTAL & GEM

26 REPTILE

27 INVENTION

28 WEATHER

29 CAT

30 BIBLE LANDS

31 EXPLORER

32 DOG

33 HORSE

34 FILM

35 COSTUME

36 BOAT

37 ANCIENT GREECE

38 VOLCANO & EARTHQUAKE

39 TRAIN

40 SHARK

41 AMPHIBIAN

42 ELEPHANT

43 KNIGHT

44 MUMMY

45 COWBOY

46 WHALE

47 AZTEC, INCA & MAYA

48 BOOK

49 CASTLE

50 VIKING

51 DESERT

52 PREHISTORIC LIFE

53 PYRAMID

54 JUNGLE

55 ANCIENT CHINA